Sex Discrimination

CHAPTER 65

ARRANGEMENT OF SECTIONS

PART I

DISCRIMINATION TO WHICH ACT APPLIES

Section
1. Sex discrimination against women.
2. Sex discrimination against men.
3. Discrimination against married persons in employment field.
4. Discrimination by way of victimisation.
5. Interpretation.

PART II

DISCRIMINATION IN THE EMPLOYMENT FIELD

Discrimination by employers

6. Discrimination against applicants and employees.
7. Exception where sex is a genuine occupational qualification.
8. Equal Pay Act 1970.
9. Discrimination against contract workers.
10. Meaning of employment at establishment in Great Britain.

Discrimination by other bodies

11. Partnerships.
12. Trade unions etc.
13. Qualifying bodies.
14. Vocational training bodies.
15. Employment agencies.
16. Manpower Services Commission etc.

Special cases

17. Police.
18. Prison officers.
19. Ministers of religion etc.
20. Midwives.
21. Mineworkers.

A

Part III

Discrimination in Other Fields

Education

Section
22. Discrimination by bodies in charge of educational establishments.
23. Other discrimination by local education authorities.
24. Designated establishments.
25. General duty in public sector of education.
26. Exception for single-sex establishments.
27. Exception for single-sex establishments turning co-educational.
28. Exception for physical training.

Goods, facilities, services and premises

29. Discrimination in provision of goods, facilities or services.
30. Discrimination in disposal or management of premises.
31. Discrimination: consent for assignment or sub-letting.
32. Exception for small dwellings.
33. Exception for political parties.
34. Exception for voluntary bodies.
35. Further exceptions from ss. 29(1) and 30.

Extent

36. Extent of Part III.

Part IV

Other Unlawful Acts

37. Discriminatory practices.
38. Discriminatory advertisements.
39. Instructions to discriminate.
40. Pressure to discriminate.
41. Liability of employers and principals.
42. Aiding unlawful acts.

Part V

General Exceptions from Parts II to IV

43. Charities.
44. Sport etc.
45. Insurance etc.
46. Communal accommodation.
47. Discriminatory training by certain bodies.
48. Other discriminatory training etc.
49. Trade unions etc.: elective bodies.
50. Indirect access to benefits etc.
51. Acts done under statutory authority.
52. Acts safeguarding national security.

Part VI
Equal Opportunities Commission
General

Section
53. Establishment and duties of Commission.
54. Research and education.
55. Review of discriminatory provisions in health and safety legislation.
56. Annual reports.

Investigations

57. Power to conduct formal investigations.
58. Terms of reference.
59. Power to obtain information.
60. Recommendations and reports on formal investigations.
61. Restriction on disclosure of information.

Part VII
Enforcement
General

62. No further sanctions for breach of Act.

Enforcement in employment field

63. Jurisdiction of industrial tribunals.
64. Conciliation in employment cases.
65. Remedies on complaint under section 63.

Enforcement of Part III

66. Claims under Part III.

Non-discrimination notices

67. Issue of non-discrimination notice.
68. Appeal against non-discrimination notice.
69. Investigation as to compliance with non-discrimination notice.
70. Register of non-discrimination notices.

Other enforcement by Commission

71. Persistent discrimination.
72. Enforcement of ss. 38 to 40.
73. Preliminary action in employment cases.

Help for persons suffering discrimination

Section
74. Help for aggrieved persons in obtaining information etc.
75. Assistance by Commission.

Period within which proceedings to be brought

76. Period within which proceedings to be brought.

Part VIII

Supplemental

77. Validity and revision of contracts.
78. Educational charities in England and Wales.
79. Educational endowments etc. to which Part VI of the Education (Scotland) Act 1962 applies.
80. Power to amend certain provisions of Act.
81. Orders.
82. General interpretation provisions.
83. Transitional and commencement provisions, amendments and repeals.
84. Financial provisions.
85. Application to Crown.
86. Government appointments outside section 6.
87. Short title and extent.

Schedules:
- Schedule 1—Equal Pay Act 1970.
- Schedule 2—Transitional exemption orders for educational admissions.
- Schedule 3—Equal Opportunities Commission.
- Schedule 4—Transitional provisions.
- Schedule 5—Minor and consequential amendments.
- Schedule 6—Further repeals.

ELIZABETH II

Sex Discrimination Act 1975

1975 CHAPTER 65

An Act to render unlawful certain kinds of sex discrimination and discrimination on the ground of marriage, and establish a Commission with the function of working towards the elimination of such discrimination and promoting equality of opportunity between men and women generally; and for related purposes.
[12th November 1975]

BE IT ENACTED by the Queen's most Excellent Majesty, by and with the advice and consent of the Lords Spiritual and Temporal, and Commons, in this present Parliament assembled, and by the authority of the same, as follows:—

PART I

DISCRIMINATION TO WHICH ACT APPLIES

1.—(1) A person discriminates against a woman in any circumstances relevant for the purposes of any provision of this Act if— Sex discrimination against women.

    (a) on the ground of her sex he treats her <u>less favourably</u> than he treats or would treat a man, or

    (b) he applies to her a requirement or condition which he applies or would apply equally to a man but—

        (i) which is such that the proportion of women who can comply with it is considerably smaller than the proportion of men who can comply with it, and

        (ii) which he cannot show to be justifiable irrespective of the sex of the person to whom it is applied, and

        (iii) which is to her detriment because she cannot comply with it.

PART I

(2) If a person treats or would treat a man differently according to the man's marital status, his treatment of a woman is for the purposes of subsection (1)(a) to be compared to his treatment of a man having the like marital status.

Sex discrimination against men.

2.—(1) Section 1, and the provisions of Parts II and III relating to sex discrimination against women, are to be read as applying equally to the treatment of men, and for that purpose shall have effect with such modifications as are requisite.

(2) In the application of subsection (1) no account shall be taken of special treatment afforded to women in connection with pregnancy or childbirth.

Discrimination against married persons in employment field.

3.—(1) A person discriminates against a married person of either sex in any circumstances relevant for the purposes of any provision of Part II if—

(a) on the ground of his or her marital status he treats that person less favourably than he treats or would treat an unmarried person of the same sex, or

(b) he applies to that person a requirement or condition which he applies or would apply equally to an unmarried person but—

(i) which is such that the proportion of married persons who can comply with it is considerably smaller than the proportion of unmarried persons of the same sex who can comply with it, and

(ii) which he cannot show to be justifiable irrespective of the marital status of the person to whom it is applied, and

(iii) which is to that person's detriment because he cannot comply with it.

(2) For the purposes of subsection (1), a provision of Part II framed with reference to discrimination against women shall be treated as applying equally to the treatment of men, and for that purpose shall have effect with such modifications as are requisite.

Discrimination by way of victimisation.

4.—(1) A person (" the discriminator ") discriminates against another person (" the person victimised ") in any circumstances relevant for the purposes of any provision of this Act if he treats the person victimised less favourably than in those circumstances he treats or would treat other persons, and does so by reason that the person victimised has—

1970 c. 41.

(a) brought proceedings against the discriminator or any other person under this Act or the Equal Pay Act 1970, or

(b) given evidence or information in connection with proceedings brought by any person against the discriminator or any other person under this Act or the Equal Pay Act 1970, or

(c) otherwise done anything under or by reference to this Act or the Equal Pay Act 1970 in relation to the discriminator or any other person, or

(d) alleged that the discriminator or any other person has committed an act which (whether or not the allegation so states) would amount to a contravention of this Act or give rise to a claim under the Equal Pay Act 1970,

or by reason that the discriminator knows the person victimised intends to do any of those things, or suspects the person victimised has done, or intends to do, any of them.

(2) Subsection (1) does not apply to treatment of a person by reason of any allegation made by him if the allegation was false and not made in good faith.

(3) For the purposes of subsection (1), a provision of Part II or III framed with reference to discrimination against women shall be treated as applying equally to the treatment of men and for that purpose shall have effect with such modifications as are requisite.

5.—(1) In this Act — *Interpretation.*
(a) references to discrimination refer to any discrimination falling within sections 1 to 4 ; and
(b) references to sex discrimination refer to any discrimination falling within section 1 or 2,

and related expressions shall be construed accordingly.

(2) In this Act—
" woman " includes a female of any age, and
" man " includes a male of any age.

(3) A comparison of the cases of persons of different sex or marital status under section 1(1) or 3(1) must be such that the relevant circumstances in the one case are the same, or not materially different, in the other.

Part II

Discrimination in the Employment Field

Discrimination by employers

6.—(1) It is unlawful for a person, in relation to employment by him at an establishment in Great Britain, to discriminate against a woman— *Discrimination against applicants and employees.*

(a) in the arrangements he makes for the purpose of determining who should be offered that employment, or

(b) in the terms on which he offers her that employment, or

(c) by refusing or deliberately omitting to offer her that employment.

(2) It is unlawful for a person, in the case of a woman employed by him at an establishment in Great Britain, to discriminate against her—

(a) in the way he affords her access to opportunities for promotion, transfer or training, or to any other benefits, facilities or services, or by refusing or deliberately omitting to afford her access to them, or

(b) by dismissing her, or subjecting her to any other detriment.

(3) Except in relation to discrimination falling within section 4, subsections (1) and (2) do not apply to employment—

(a) for the purposes of a private household, or

(b) where the number of persons employed by the employer, added to the number employed by any associated employers of his, does not exceed five (disregarding any persons employed for the purposes of a private household).

(4) Subsections (1)(b) and (2) do not apply to provision in relation to death or retirement.

(5) Subject to section 8(3), subsection (1)(b) does not apply to any provision for the payment of money which, if the woman in question were given the employment, would be included (directly or by reference to a collective agreement or otherwise) in the contract under which she was employed.

(6) Subsection (2) does not apply to benefits consisting of the payment of money when the provision of those benefits is regulated by the woman's contract of employment.

(7) Subsection (2) does not apply to benefits, facilities or services of any description if the employer is concerned with the provision (for payment or not) of benefits, facilities or services of that description to the public, or to a section of the public comprising the woman in question, unless—

(a) that provision differs in a material respect from the provision of the benefits, facilities or services by the employer to his employees, or

(b) the provision of the benefits, facilities or services to the woman in question is regulated by her contract of employment, or

(c) the benefits, facilities or services relate to training.

7.—(1) In relation to sex discrimination—

(*a*) section 6(1)(*a*) or (*c*) does not apply to any employment where being a man is a genuine occupational qualification for the job, and

(*b*) section 6(2)(*a*) does not apply to opportunities for promotion or transfer to, or training for, such employment.

<small>PART II

Exception where sex is a genuine occupational qualification.</small>

(2) Being a man is a genuine occupational qualification for a job only where—

(*a*) the essential nature of the job calls for a man for reasons of physiology (excluding physical strength or stamina) or, in dramatic performances or other entertainment, for reasons of authenticity, so that the essential nature of the job would be materially different if carried out by a woman; or

(*b*) the job needs to be held by a man to preserve decency or privacy because—

(i) it is likely to involve physical contact with men in circumstances where they might reasonably object to its being carried out by a woman, or

(ii) the holder of the job is likely to do his work in circumstances where men might reasonably object to the presence of a woman because they are in a state of undress or are using sanitary facilities; or

(*c*) the nature or location of the establishment makes it impracticable for the holder of the job to live elsewhere than in premises provided by the employer, and—

(i) the only such premises which are available for persons holding that kind of job are lived in, or normally lived in, by men and are not equipped with separate sleeping accommodation for women and sanitary facilities which could be used by women in privacy from men, and

(ii) it is not reasonable to expect the employer either to equip those premises with such accommodation and facilities or to provide other premises for women; or

(*d*) the nature of the establishment, or of the part of it within which the work is done, requires the job to be held by a man because—

(i) it is, or is part of, a hospital, prison or other establishment for persons requiring special care, supervision or attention, and

(ii) those persons are all men (disregarding any woman whose presence is exceptional), and

PART II

    (iii) it is reasonable, having regard to the essential character of the establishment or that part, that the job should not be held by a woman; or

 (e) the holder of the job provides individuals with personal services promoting their welfare or education, or similar personal services, and those services can most effectively be provided by a man, or

 (f) the job needs to be held by a man because of restrictions imposed by the laws regulating the employment of women, or

 (g) the job needs to be held by a man because it is likely to involve the performance of duties outside the United Kingdom in a country whose laws or customs are such that the duties could not, or could not effectively, be performed by a woman, or

 (h) the job is one of two to be held by a married couple.

(3) Subsection (2) applies where some only of the duties of the job fall within paragraphs (a) to (g) as well as where all of them do.

(4) Paragraph (a), (b), (c), (d), (e), (f) or (g) of subsection (2) does not apply in relation to the filling of a vacancy at a time when the employer already has male employees—

 (a) who are capable of carrying out the duties falling within that paragraph, and

 (b) whom it would be reasonable to employ on those duties, and

 (c) whose numbers are sufficient to meet the employer's likely requirements in respect of those duties without undue inconvenience.

Equal Pay Act 1970.
1970 c. 41.

8.—(1) In section 1 of the Equal Pay Act 1970, the following are substituted for subsections (1) to (3)—

 " (1) If the terms of a contract under which a woman is employed at an establishment in Great Britain do not include (directly or by reference to a collective agreement or otherwise) an equality clause they shall be deemed to include one.

 (2) An equality clause is a provision which relates to terms (whether concerned with pay or not) of a contract under which a woman is employed (the " woman's contract "), and has the effect that—

 (a) where the woman is employed on like work with a man in the same employment—

  (i) if (apart from the equality clause) any term of the woman's contract is or becomes less favourable to the woman than a term of a similar kind in the contract under which that man is employed, that term of the woman's contract shall be treated as so modified as not to be less favourable, and

(ii) if (apart from the equality clause) at any time the woman's contract does not include a term corresponding to a term benefiting that man included in the contract under which he is employed, the woman's contract shall be treated as including such a term;

(b) where the woman is employed on work rated as equivalent with that of a man in the same employment—

(i) if (apart from the equality clause) any term of the woman's contract determined by the rating of the work is or becomes less favourable to the woman than a term of a similar kind in the contract under which that man is employed, that term of the woman's contract shall be treated as so modified as not to be less favourable, and

(ii) if (apart from the equality clause) at any time the woman's contract does not include a term corresponding to a term benefiting that man included in the contract under which he is employed and determined by the rating of the work, the woman's contract shall be treated as including such a term.

(3) An equality clause shall not operate in relation to a variation between the woman's contract and the man's contract if the employer proves that the variation is genuinely due to a material difference (other than the difference of sex) between her case and his."

(2) Section 1(1) of the Equal Pay Act 1970 (as set out in subsection (1) above) does not apply in determining for the purposes of section 6(1)(b) of this Act the terms on which employment is offered.

1970 c. 41.

(3) Where a person offers a woman employment on certain terms, and if she accepted the offer then, by virtue of an equality clause, any of those terms would fall to be modified, or any additional term would fall to be included, the offer shall be taken to contravene section 6(1)(b).

(4) Where a person offers a woman employment on certain terms, and subsection (3) would apply but for the fact that, on her acceptance of the offer, section 1(3) of the Equal Pay Act 1970 (as set out in subsection (1) above) would prevent the equality clause from operating, the offer shall be taken not to contravene section 6(1)(b).

PART II

(5) An act does not contravene section 6(2) if—
  (a) it contravenes a term modified or included by virtue of an equality clause, or
  (b) it would contravene such a term but for the fact that the equality clause is prevented from operating by section 1(3) of the Equal Pay Act 1970.

1970 c. 41.

(6) The Equal Pay Act 1970 is further amended as specified in Part I of Schedule 1, and accordingly has effect as set out in Part II of Schedule 1.

Discrimination against contract workers.

9.—(1) This section applies to any work for a person ("the principal") which is available for doing by individuals ("contract workers") who are employed not by the principal himself but by another person, who supplies them under a contract made with the principal.

(2) It is unlawful for the principal, in relation to work to which this section applies, to discriminate against a woman who is a contract worker—
  (a) in the terms on which he allows her to do that work, or
  (b) by not allowing her to do it or continue to do it, or
  (c) in the way he affords her access to any benefits, facilities or services or by refusing or deliberately omitting to afford her access to them, or
  (d) by subjecting her to any other detriment.

(3) The principal does not contravene subsection (2)(b) by doing any act in relation to a woman at a time when if the work were to be done by a person taken into his employment being a man would be a genuine occupational qualification for the job.

(4) Subsection (2)(c) does not apply to benefits, facilities or services of any description if the principal is concerned with the provision (for payment or not) of benefits, facilities or services of that description to the public, or to a section of the public to which the woman belongs, unless that provision differs in a material respect from the provision of the benefits, facilities or services by the principal to his contract workers.

Meaning of employment at establishment in Great Britain.

10.—(1) For the purposes of this Part and section 1 of the Equal Pay Act 1970 ("the relevant purposes"), employment is to be regarded as being at an establishment in Great Britain unless the employee does his work wholly or mainly outside Great Britain.

(2) Subsection (1) does not apply to—
  (a) employment on board a ship registered at a port of registry in Great Britain, or

(b) employment on aircraft or hovercraft registered in the United Kingdom and operated by a person who has his principal place of business, or is ordinarily resident, in Great Britain;

PART II

but for the relevant purposes such employment is to be regarded as being at an establishment in Great Britain unless the employee does his work wholly outside Great Britain.

(3) In the case of employment on board a ship registered at a port of registry in Great Britain (except where the employee does his work wholly outside Great Britain, and outside any area added under subsection (5)) the ship shall for the relevant purposes be deemed to be the establishment.

(4) Where work is not done at an establishment it shall be treated for the relevant purposes as done at the establishment from which it is done or (where it is not done from any establishment) at the establishment with which it has the closest connection.

(5) In relation to employment concerned with exploration of the sea bed or subsoil or the exploitation of their natural resources, Her Majesty may by Order in Council provide that subsections (1) and (2) shall each have effect as if the last reference to Great Britain included any area for the time being designated under section 1(7) of the Continental Shelf Act 1964, except an area or part of an area in which the law of Northern Ireland applies.

1964 c. 29.

(6) An Order in Council under subsection (5) may provide that, in relation to employment to which the Order applies, this Part and section 1 of the Equal Pay Act 1970 are to have effect with such modifications as are specified in the Order.

1970 c. 41.

(7) An Order in Council under subsection (5) shall be of no effect unless a draft of the Order was laid before and approved by each House of Parliament.

Discrimination by other bodies

11.—(1) It is unlawful for a firm consisting of six or more partners, in relation to a position as partner in the firm, to discriminate against a woman—

Partnerships.

    (a) in the arrangements they make for the purpose of determining who should be offered that position, or

    (b) in the terms on which they offer her that position, or

    (c) by refusing or deliberately omitting to offer her that position, or

    (d) in a case where the woman already holds that position—

        (i) in the way they afford her access to any benefits, facilities or services, or by refusing or deliberately omitting to afford her access to them, or

PART II

(ii) by expelling her from that position, or subjecting her to any other detriment.

(2) Subsection (1) shall apply in relation to persons proposing to form themselves into a partnership as it applies in relation to a firm.

(3) Subsection (1)(a) and (c) do not apply to a position as partner where, if it were employment, being a man would be a genuine occupational qualification for the job.

(4) Subsection (1)(b) and (d) do not apply to provision made in relation to death or retirement.

1907 c. 24.

(5) In the case of a limited partnership references in subsection (1) to a partner shall be construed as references to a general partner as defined in section 3 of the Limited Partnerships Act 1907.

Trade unions etc.

12.—(1) This section applies to an organisation of workers, an organisation of employers, or any other organisation whose members carry on a particular profession or trade for the purposes of which the organisation exists.

(2) It is unlawful for an organisation to which this section applies, in the case of a woman who is not a member of the organisation, to discriminate against her—

    (a) in the terms on which it is prepared to admit her to membership, or

    (b) by refusing, or deliberately omitting to accept, her application for membership.

(3) It is unlawful for an organisation to which this section applies, in the case of a woman who is a member of the organisation, to discriminate against her—

    (a) in the way it affords her access to any benefits, facilities or services, or by refusing or deliberately omitting to afford her access to them, or

    (b) by depriving her of membership, or varying the terms on which she is a member, or

    (c) by subjecting her to any other detriment.

(4) This section does not apply to provision made in relation to the death or retirement from work of a member.

Qualifying bodies.

13.—(1) It is unlawful for an authority or body which can confer an authorisation or qualification which is needed for, or facilitates, engagement in a particular profession or trade to discriminate against a woman—

    (a) in the terms on which it is prepared to confer on her that authorisation or qualification, or

(b) by refusing or deliberately omitting to grant her application for it, or

(c) by withdrawing it from her or varying the terms on which she holds it.

(2) Where an authority or body is required by law to satisfy itself as to his good character before conferring on a person an authorisation or qualification which is needed for, or facilitates, his engagement in any profession or trade then, without prejudice to any other duty to which it is subject, that requirement shall be taken to impose on the authority or body a duty to have regard to any evidence tending to show that he, or any of his employees, or agents (whether past or present), has practised unlawful discrimination in, or in connection with, the carrying on of any profession or trade.

(3) In this section—
  (a) " authorisation or qualification " includes recognition, registration, enrolment, approval and certification,
  (b) " confer " includes renew or extend.

(4) Subsection (1) does not apply to discrimination which is rendered unlawful by section 22 or 23.

14.—(1) It is unlawful for a person to whom this subsection applies, in the case of a woman seeking or undergoing training which would help to fit her for any employment, to discriminate against her—   *Vocational training bodies.*
  (a) in the terms on which that person affords her access to any training courses or other facilities, or
  (b) by refusing or deliberately omitting to afford her such access, or
  (c) by terminating her training.

(2) Subsection (1) applies to—
  (a) industrial training boards established under section 1 of the Industrial Training Act 1964;   *1964 c. 16.*
  (b) the Manpower Services Commission, the Employment Service Agency, and the Training Services Agency;
  (c) any association which comprises employers and has as its principal object, or one of its principal objects, affording their employees access to training facilities;
  (d) any other person providing facilities for training for employment, being a person designated for the purposes of this paragraph in an order made by or on behalf of the Secretary of State.

(3) Subsection (1) does not apply to discrimination which is rendered unlawful by section 22 or 23.

PART II
Employment
agencies.

15.—(1) It is unlawful for an employment agency to discriminate against a woman—
  (a) in the terms on which the agency offers to provide any of its services, or
  (b) by refusing or deliberately omitting to provide any of its services, or
  (c) in the way it provides any of its services.

1973 c. 50.

(2) It is unlawful for a local education authority or an education authority to do any act in the performance of its functions under section 8 of the Employment and Training Act 1973 which constitutes discrimination.

(3) References in subsection (1) to the services of an employment agency include guidance on careers and any other services related to employment.

(4) This section does not apply if the discrimination only concerns employment which the employer could lawfully refuse to offer the woman.

(5) An employment agency or local education authority or an education authority shall not be subject to any liability under this section if it proves—
  (a) that it acted in reliance on a statement made to it by the employer to the effect that, by reason of the operation of subsection (4), its action would not be unlawful, and
  (b) that it was reasonable for it to rely on the statement.

(6) A person who knowingly or recklessly makes a statement such as is referred to in subsection (5)(a) which in a material respect is false or misleading commits an offence, and shall be liable on summary conviction to a fine not exceeding £400.

Manpower
Services
Commission
etc.

16.—(1) It is unlawful for any of the following bodies to discriminate in the provision of facilities or services under section 2 of the Employment and Training Act 1973—
  (a) the Manpower Services Commission;
  (b) the Employment Service Agency;
  (c) the Training Services Agency.

(2) This section does not apply in a case where—
  (a) section 14 applies, or
  (b) the body is acting as an employment agency.

Special cases PART II

Police.
17.—(1) For the purposes of this Part, the holding of the office of constable shall be treated as employment—

(a) by the chief officer of police as respects any act done by him in relation to a constable or that office;

(b) by the police authority as respects any act done by them in relation to a constable or that office.

(2) Regulations made under section 33, 34 or 35 of the Police 1964 c. 48. Act 1964 shall not treat men and women differently except—

(a) as to requirements relating to height, uniform or equipment, or allowances in lieu of uniform or equipment, or

(b) so far as special treatment is accorded to women in connection with pregnancy or childbirth, or

(c) in relation to pensions to or in respect of special constables or police cadets.

(3) Nothing in this Part renders unlawful any discrimination between male and female constables as to matters such as are mentioned in subsection (2)(a).

(4) There shall be paid out of the police fund—

(a) any compensation, costs or expenses awarded against a chief officer of police in any proceedings brought against him under this Act, and any costs or expenses incurred by him in any such proceedings so far as not recovered by him in the proceedings; and

(b) any sum required by a chief officer of police for the settlement of any claim made against him under this Act if the settlement is approved by the police authority.

(5) Any proceedings under this Act which, by virtue of subsection (1), would lie against a chief officer of police shall be brought against the chief officer of police for the time being or, in the case of a vacancy in that office, against the person for the time being performing the functions of that office; and references in subsection (4) to the chief officer of police shall be construed accordingly.

(6) Subsections (1) and (3) apply to a police cadet and appointment as a police cadet as they apply to a constable and the office of constable.

(7) In this section—

" chief officer of police "—

(a) in relation to a person appointed, or an appointment falling to be made, under a specified Act,

A 7

PART II
1964 c. 48.

has the same meaning as in the Police Act 1964,

(b) in relation to any other person or appointment means the officer who has the direction and control of the body of constables or cadets in question;

" police authority "—

(a) in relation to a person appointed, or an appointment falling to be made, under a specified Act, has the same meaning as in the Police Act 1964,

(b) in relation to any other person or appointment, means the authority by whom the person in question is or on appointment would be paid;

" police cadet " means any person appointed to undergo training with a view to becoming a constable;

" police fund " in relation to a chief officer of police within paragraph (a) of the above definition of that term has the same meaning as in the Police Act 1964, and in any other case means money provided by the police authority;

1829 c. 44.
1839 c. xciv.

" specified Act " means the Metropolitan Police Act 1829, the City of London Police Act 1839 or the Police Act 1964.

1967 c. 77.

(8) In the application of this section to Scotland, in subsection (7) for any reference to the Police Act 1964 there shall be substituted a reference to the Police (Scotland) Act 1967, and for the reference to sections 33, 34 and 35 of the former Act in subsection (2) there shall be substituted a reference to sections 26 and 27 of the latter Act.

Prison officers. **18.**—(1) Nothing in this Part renders unlawful any discrimination between male and female prison officers as to requirements relating to height.

1952 c. 52.

(2) In section 7(2) of the Prison Act 1952 the words " and if women only are received in a prison the Governor shall be a woman " are repealed.

Ministers of religion etc.

19.—(1) Nothing in this Part applies to employment for purposes of an organised religion where the employment is limited to one sex so as to comply with the doctrines of the religion or avoid offending the religious susceptibilities of a significant number of its followers.

(2) Nothing in section 13 applies to an authorisation or qualification (as defined in that section) for purposes of an organised religion where the authorisation or qualification is limited to one sex so as to comply with the doctrines of the religion or avoid offending the religious susceptibilities of a significant number of its followers.

20.—(1) Section 6(1) does not apply to employment as a midwife.

PART II
Midwives.

(2) Section 6(2)(*a*) does not apply to promotion, transfer or training as a midwife.

(3) Section 14 does not apply to training as a midwife.

(4) In the Midwives Act 1951 the following section is inserted after section 35—

1951 c. 53.

"Extension of Act to men.

35A. From 1st January 1976 references in this Act to women (except to a woman in childbirth) apply equally to men."

(5) In the Midwives (Scotland) Act 1951 the said section 35A is inserted after section 37 of that Act as section 37A.

1951 c. 54.

21.—(1) The following shall be substituted for section 124(1) of the Mines and Quarries Act 1954 (which provides that no female shall be employed below ground at a mine)—

Mineworkers.
1954 c. 70.

"(1) No female shall be employed in a job the duties of which ordinarily require the employee to spend a significant proportion of his time below ground at a mine which is being worked"

(2) Throughout the Coal Mines Regulation Act 1908, for "workman" or "man" there is substituted "worker", and for "workmen" or "men" there is substituted "workers".

1908 c. 57.

PART III

DISCRIMINATION IN OTHER FIELDS

Education

22. It is unlawful in relation to an educational establishment falling within column 1 of the following table, for a person indicated in relation to the establishment in column 2 (the "responsible body") to discriminate against a woman—

Discrimination by bodies in charge of educational establishments.

   (*a*) in the terms on which it offers to admit her to the establishment as a pupil, or

   (*b*) by refusing or deliberately omitting to accept an application for her admission to the establishment as a pupil, or

   (*c*) where she is a pupil of the establishment—

      (i) in the way it affords her access to any benefits, facilities or services, or by refusing or deliberately omitting to afford her access to them, or

      (ii) by excluding her from the establishment or subjecting her to any other detriment.

TABLE

Establishment	Responsible body
ENGLAND AND WALES	
1. Educational establishment maintained by a local education authority.	Local education authority or managers or governors, according to which of them has the function in question.
2. Independent school not being a special school.	Proprietor.
3. Special school not maintained by a local education authority.	Proprietor.
4. University.	Governing body.
5. Establishment (not falling within paragraphs 1 to 4) providing full-time or part-time education, being an establishment designated under section 24(1).	Governing body.
SCOTLAND	
6. Educational establishment managed by an education authority.	Education authority.
7. Educational establishment in respect of which the managers are for the time being receiving grants under section 75(c) or (d) of the Education (Scotland) Act 1962.	Managers of the educational establishment.
8. University.	Governing body.
9. Independent school.	Proprietor.
10. Any other educational establishment (not falling within paragraphs 6, 7 and 9) providing full or part-time school education or further education.	Managers of the educational establishment.

1962 c. 47.

Other discrimination by local education authorities.

23.—(1) It is unlawful for a local education authority, in carrying out such of its functions under the Education Acts 1944 to 1975 as do not fall under section 22, to do any act which constitutes sex discrimination.

(2) It is unlawful for an education authority, in carrying out such of its functions under the Education (Scotland) Acts 1939 to 1974 as do not fall under section 22, to do any act which constitutes sex discrimination.

PART III

24.—(1) The Secretary of State may by order designate for the purposes of paragraph 5 of the table in section 22 such establishments of the description mentioned in that paragraph as he thinks fit.

Designated establishments.

(2) An establishment shall not be designated under subsection (1) unless—
  (a) it is recognised by the Secretary of State as a polytechnic, or
  (b) it is an establishment in respect of which grants are payable out of money provided by Parliament, or
  (c) it is assisted by a local education authority in accordance with a scheme approved under section 42 of the Education Act 1944, or
  (d) it provides full-time education for persons who have attained the upper limit of compulsory school age but not the age of nineteen.

1944 c. 31.

(3) A designation under subsection (1) shall remain in force until revoked notwithstanding that the establishment ceases to be within subsection (2).

25.—(1) Without prejudice to its obligation to comply with any other provision of this Act, a body to which this subsection applies shall be under a general duty to secure that facilities for education provided by it, and any ancillary benefits or services, are provided without sex discrimination.

General duty in public sector of education.

(2) The following provisions of the Education Act 1944, namely—
  (a) section 68 (power of Secretary of State to require duties under that Act to be exercised reasonably), and
  (b) section 99 (powers of Secretary of State where local education authorities etc. are in default),
shall apply to the performance by a body to which subsection (1) applies of the duties imposed by sections 22 and 23 and shall also apply to the performance of the general duty imposed by subsection (1), as they apply to the performance by a local education authority of a duty imposed by that Act.

(3) Section 71 of the Education (Scotland) Act 1962 (power of the Secretary of State to require duties in that Act to be exercised) shall apply to the performance by a body to which subsection (1) applies of the duties imposed by sections 22 and 23 and shall

1962 c. 47.

PART III also apply to the performance of the general duty imposed by subsection (1), as the said section 71 applies to the performance by an education authority of a duty imposed by that Act.

(4) The sanctions in subsections (2) and (3) shall be the only sanctions for breach of the general duty in subsection (1), but without prejudice to the enforcement of sections 22 and 23 under section 66 or otherwise (where the breach is also a contravention of either of those sections).

1962 c. 47. (5) The Secretary of State shall have the power to cause a local inquiry to be held into any matter arising from subsection (3) under section 68 of the Education (Scotland) Act 1962.

(6) Subsection (1) applies to—

(a) local education authorities in England and Wales;
(b) education authorities in Scotland;
(c) any other body which is a responsible body in relation to—

(i) an establishment falling within paragraph 1, 3 or 7 of the table in section 22;

(ii) an establishment designated under section 24(1) as falling within paragraph (a) or (c) of section 24(2);

1944 c. 31. (iii) an establishment designated under section 24(1) as falling within paragraph (b) of section 24(2) where the grants in question are payable under section 100 of the Education Act 1944.

Exception for single-sex establishments. **26.**—(1) Sections 22(a) and (b) and 25 do not apply to the admission of pupils to any establishment (a " single-sex establishment ") which admits pupils of one sex only, or which would be taken to admit pupils of one sex only if there were disregarded pupils of the opposite sex—

(a) whose admission is exceptional, or
(b) whose numbers are comparatively small and whose admission is confined to particular courses of instruction or teaching classes.

(2) Where a school which is not a single-sex establishment has some pupils as boarders and others as non-boarders, and admits as boarders pupils of one sex only (or would be taken to admit as boarders pupils of one sex only if there were disregarded boarders of the opposite sex whose numbers are comparatively small), sections 22(a) and (b) and 25 do not apply to the admission of boarders and sections 22(c)(i) and 25 do not apply to boarding facilities.

(3) Where an establishment is a single-sex establishment by reason of its inclusion in subsection (1)(*b*), the fact that pupils of one sex are confined to particular courses of instruction or teaching classes shall not be taken to contravene section 22(*c*)(i) or the duty in section 25.

27.—(1) Where at any time—

(*a*) the responsible body for a single-sex establishment falling within column 1 of the table in section 22 determines to alter its admissions arrangements so that the establishment will cease to be a single-sex establishment, or

(*b*) section 26(2) applies to the admission of boarders to a school falling within column 1 of that table but the responsible body determines to alter its admissions arrangements so that section 26(2) will cease so to apply,

the responsible body may apply in accordance with Schedule 2 for an order (a "transitional exemption order") authorising discriminatory admissions during the transitional period specified in the order.

Exception for single-sex establishments turning co-educational.

(2) Where during the transitional period specified in a transitional exemption order applying to an establishment the responsible body refuses or deliberately omits to accept an application for the admission of a person to the establishment as a pupil the refusal or omission shall not be taken to contravene any provision of this Act.

(3) Subsection (2) does not apply if the refusal or omission contravenes any condition of the transitional exemption order.

(4) Except as mentioned in subsection (2), a transitional exemption order shall not afford any exemption from liability under this Act.

(5) Where, during the period between the making of an application for a transitional exemption order in relation to an establishment and the determination of the application, the responsible body refuses or deliberately omits to accept an application for the admission of a person to the establishment as a pupil the refusal or omission shall not be taken to contravene any provision of this Act.

28. Sections 22, 23 and 25 do not apply to any further education course being—

(*a*) a course in physical training, or

(*b*) a course designed for teachers of physical training.

Exception for physical training.

PART III

Goods, facilities, services and premises

Discrimination in provision of goods, facilities or services.

29.—(1) It is unlawful for any person concerned with the provision (for payment or not) of goods, facilities or services to the public or a section of the public to discriminate against a woman who seeks to obtain or use those goods, facilities or services—

(a) by refusing or deliberately omitting to provide her with any of them, or

(b) by refusing or deliberately omitting to provide her with goods, facilities or services of the like quality, in the like manner and on the like terms as are normal in his case in relation to male members of the public or (where she belongs to a section of the public) to male members of that section.

(2) The following are examples of the facilities and services mentioned in subsection (1)—

(a) access to and use of any place which members of the public or a section of the public are permitted to enter;

(b) accommodation in a hotel, boarding house or other similar establishment;

(c) facilities by way of banking or insurance or for grants, loans, credit or finance;

(d) facilities for education;

(e) facilities for entertainment, recreation or refreshment;

(f) facilities for transport or travel;

(g) the services of any profession or trade, or any local or other public authority.

(3) For the avoidance of doubt it is hereby declared that where a particular skill is commonly exercised in a different way for men and for women it does not contravene subsection (1) for a person who does not normally exercise it for women to insist on exercising it for a woman only in accordance with his normal practice or, if he reasonably considers it impracticable to do that in her case, to refuse or deliberately omit to exercise it.

Discrimination in disposal or management of premises.

30.—(1) It is unlawful for a person, in relation to premises in Great Britain of which he has power to dispose, to discriminate against a woman—

(a) in the terms on which he offers her those premises, or

(b) by refusing her application for those premises, or

(c) in his treatment of her in relation to any list of persons in need of premises of that description.

(2) It is unlawful for a person, in relation to premises managed by him, to discriminate against a woman occupying the premises—

 (a) in the way he affords her access to any benefits or facilities, or by refusing or deliberately omitting to afford her access to them, or

 (b) by evicting her, or subjecting her to any other detriment.

(3) Subsection (1) does not apply to a person who owns an estate or interest in the premises and wholly occupies them unless he uses the services of an estate agent for the purposes of the disposal of the premises, or publishes or causes to be published an advertisement in connection with the disposal.

31.—(1) Where the licence or consent of the landlord or of any other person is required for the disposal to any person of premises in Great Britain comprised in a tenancy, it is unlawful for the landlord or other person to discriminate against a woman by withholding the licence or consent for disposal of the premises to her.

Discrimination: consent for assignment or sub-letting.

(2) Subsection (1) does not apply if—

 (a) the person withholding a licence or consent, or a near relative of his ("the relevant occupier") resides, and intends to continue to reside, on the premises, and

 (b) there is on the premises, in addition to the accommodation occupied by the relevant occupier, accommodation (not being storage accommodation or means of access) shared by the relevant occupier with other persons residing on the premises who are not members of his household, and

 (c) the premises are small premises as defined in section 32(2).

(3) In this section "tenancy" means a tenancy created by a lease or sub-lease, by an agreement for a lease or sub-lease or by a tenancy agreement or in pursuance of any enactment; and "disposal", in relation to premises comprised in a tenancy, includes assignment or assignation of the tenancy and sub-letting or parting with possession of the premises or any part of the premises.

(4) This section applies to tenancies created before the passing of this Act, as well as to others.

32.—(1) Sections 29(1) and 30 do not apply to the provision by a person of accommodation in any premises, or the disposal of premises by him, if—

Exception for small dwellings.

 (a) that person or a near relative of his ("the relevant occupier") resides, and intends to continue to reside, on the premises, and

(b) there is on the premises, in addition to the accommodation occupied by the relevant occupier, accommodation (not being storage accommodation or means of access) shared by the relevant occupier with other persons residing on the premises who are not members of his household, and

(c) the premises are small premises.

(2) Premises shall be treated for the purposes of subsection (1) as small premises if—

(a) in the case of premises comprising residential accommodation for one or more households (under separate letting or similar agreements) in addition to the accommodation occupied by the relevant occupier, there is not normally residential accommodation for more than two such households and only the relevant occupier and any member of his household reside in the accommodation occupied by him;

(b) in the case of premises not falling within paragraph (a), there is not normally residential accommodation on the premises for more than six persons in addition to the relevant occupier and any members of his household.

Exception for political parties.

33.—(1) This section applies to a political party if—

(a) it has as its main object, or one of its main objects, the promotion of parliamentary candidatures for the Parliament of the United Kingdom, or

(b) it is an affiliate of, or has as an affiliate, or has similar formal links with, a political party within paragraph (a).

(2) Nothing in section 29(1) shall be construed as affecting any special provision for persons of one sex only in the constitution, organisation or administration of the political party.

(3) Nothing in section 29(1) shall render unlawful an act done in order to give effect to such a special provision.

Exception for voluntary bodies.

34.—(1) This section applies to a body—

(a) the activities of which are carried on otherwise than for profit, and

(b) which was not set up by any enactment.

(2) Sections 29(1) and 30 shall not be construed as rendering unlawful—

(a) the restriction of membership of any such body to persons of one sex (disregarding any minor exceptions), or

(b) the provision of benefits, facilities or services to members of any such body where the membership is so restricted,

even though membership of the body is open to the public, or to a section of the public.

(3) Nothing in section 29 or 30 shall—
  (a) be construed as affecting a provision to which this subsection applies, or
  (b) render unlawful an act which is done in order to give effect to such a provision.

(4) Subsection (3) applies to a provision for conferring benefits on persons of one sex only (disregarding any benefits to persons of the opposite sex which are exceptional or are relatively insignificant), being a provision which constitutes the main object of a body within subsection (1).

35.—(1) A person who provides at any place facilities or services restricted to men does not for that reason contravene section 29(1) if—

Further exceptions from ss. 29(1) and 30.

  (a) the place is, or is part of, a hospital, reception centre provided by the Supplementary Benefits Commission or other establishment for persons requiring special care, supervision or attention, or
  (b) the place is (permanently or for the time being) occupied or used for the purposes of an organised religion, and the facilities or services are restricted to men so as to comply with the doctrines of that religion or avoid offending the religious susceptibilities of a significant number of its followers, or
  (c) the facilities or services are provided for, or are likely to be used by, two or more persons at the same time, and
    (i) the facilities or services are such, or those persons are such, that male users are likely to suffer serious embarrassment at the presence of a woman, or
    (ii) the facilities or services are such that a user is likely to be in a state of undress and a male user might reasonably object to the presence of a female user.

(2) A person who provides facilities or services restricted to men does not for that reason contravene section 29(1) if the services or facilities are such that physical contact between the user and any other person is likely, and that other person might reasonably object if the user were a woman.

(3) Sections 29(1) and 30 do not apply—
- (a) to discrimination which is rendered unlawful by any provision in column 1 of the table below, or
- (b) to discrimination which would be so unlawful but for any provision in column 2 of that table, or
- (c) to discrimination which contravenes a term modified or included by virtue of an equality clause.

TABLE

Provision creating illegality	Exception
Part II	Sections 6(3), 7(1)(b), 15(4), 19 and 20. Schedule 4 paragraphs 1 and 2.
Section 22 or 23	Sections 26, 27 and 28. Schedule 4 paragraph 4.

Extent

36.—(1) Section 29(1)—
- (a) does not apply to goods, facilities or services outside Great Britain except as provided in subsections (2) and (3), and
- (b) does not apply to facilities by way of banking or insurance or for grants, loans, credit or finance, where the facilities are for a purpose to be carried out, or in connection with risks wholly or mainly arising, outside Great Britain.

(2) Section 29(1) applies to the provision of facilities for travel outside Great Britain where the refusal or omission occurs in Great Britain or on a ship, aircraft or hovercraft within subsection (3).

(3) Section 29(1) applies on and in relation to—
- (a) any ship registered at a port of registry in Great Britain, and
- (b) any aircraft or hovercraft registered in the United Kingdom and operated by a person who has his principal place of business, or is ordinarily resident, in Great Britain,
- (c) any ship, aircraft or hovercraft belonging to or possessed by Her Majesty in right of the Government of the United Kingdom,

even if the ship, aircraft or hovercraft is outside Great Britain.

(4) This section shall not render unlawful an act done in or over a country outside the United Kingdom, or in or over that country's territorial waters, for the purpose of complying with the laws of that country.

(5) Sections 22, 23 and 25 do not apply to benefits, facilities or services outside Great Britain except—

(*a*) travel on a ship registered at a port of registry in Great Britain, and

(*b*) benefits, facilities or services provided on a ship so registered.

PART IV
OTHER UNLAWFUL ACTS

37.—(1) In this section " discriminatory practice " means the application of a requirement or condition which results in an act of discrimination which is unlawful by virtue of any provision of Part II or III taken with section 1(1)(*b*) or 3(1)(*b*) or which would be likely to result in such an act of discrimination if the persons to whom it is applied were not all of one sex.

Discriminatory practices.

(2) A person acts in contravention of this section if and so long as—

(*a*) he applies a discriminatory practice, or

(*b*) he operates practices or other arrangements which in any circumstances would call for the application by him of a discriminatory practice.

(3) Proceedings in respect of a contravention of this section shall be brought only by the Commission in accordance with sections 67 to 71.

38.—(1) It is unlawful to publish or cause to be published an advertisement which indicates, or might reasonably be understood as indicating, an intention by a person to do any act which is or might be unlawful by virtue of Part II or III.

Discriminatory advertisements.

(2) Subsection (1) does not apply to an advertisement if the intended act would not in fact be unlawful.

(3) For the purposes of subsection (1), use of a job description with a sexual connotation (such as " waiter ", " salesgirl ", " postman " or " stewardess ") shall be taken to indicate an intention to discriminate, unless the advertisement contains an indication to the contrary.

(4) The publisher of an advertisement made unlawful by subsection (1) shall not be subject to any liability under that subsection in respect of the publication of the advertisement if he proves—

(*a*) that the advertisement was published in reliance on a statement made to him by the person who caused it

PART IV

to be published to the effect that, by reason of the operation of subsection (2), the publication would not be unlawful, and

(b) that it was reasonable for him to rely on the statement.

(5) A person who knowingly or recklessly makes a statement such as is referred to in subsection (4) which in a material respect is false or misleading commits an offence, and shall be liable on summary conviction to a fine not exceeding £400.

Instructions to discriminate.

39. It is unlawful for a person—

(a) who has authority over another person, or

(b) in accordance with whose wishes that other person is accustomed to act,

to instruct him to do any act which is unlawful by virtue of Part II or III, or procure or attempt to procure the doing by him of any such act.

Pressure to discriminate.

40.—(1) It is unlawful to induce, or attempt to induce, a person to do any act which contravenes Part II or III by—

(a) providing or offering to provide him with any benefit, or

(b) subjecting or threatening to subject him to any detriment.

(2) An offer or threat is not prevented from falling within subsection (1) because it is not made directly to the person in question, if it is made in such a way that he is likely to hear of it.

Liability of employers and principals.

41.—(1) Anything done by a person in the course of his employment shall be treated for the purposes of this Act as done by his employer as well as by him, whether or not it was done with the employer's knowledge or approval.

(2) Anything done by a person as agent for another person with the authority (whether express or implied, and whether precedent or subsequent) of that other person shall be treated for the purposes of this Act as done by that other person as well as by him.

(3) In proceedings brought under this Act against any person in respect of an act alleged to have been done by an employee of his it shall be a defence for that person to prove that he took such steps as were reasonably practicable to prevent the employee from doing that act, or from doing in the course of his employment acts of that description.

Aiding unlawful acts.

42.—(1) A person who knowingly aids another person to do an act made unlawful by this Act shall be treated for the purposes of this Act as himself doing an unlawful act of the like description.

(2) For the purposes of subsection (1) an employee or agent for whose act the employer or principal is liable under section 41 (or would be so liable but for section 41(3)) shall be deemed to aid the doing of the act by the employer or principal.

(3) A person does not under this section knowingly aid another to do an unlawful act if—
   (a) he acts in reliance on a statement made to him by that other person that, by reason of any provision of this Act, the act which he aids would not be unlawful, and
   (b) it is reasonable for him to rely on the statement.

(4) A person who knowingly or recklessly makes a statement such as is referred to in subsection (3)(a) which in a material respect is false or misleading commits an offence, and shall be liable on summary conviction to a fine not exceeding £400.

Part V

General Exceptions from Parts II to IV

43.—(1) Nothing in Parts II to IV shall—
   (a) be construed as affecting a provision to which this subsection applies, or
   (b) render unlawful an act which is done in order to give effect to such a provision.

(2) Subsection (1) applies to a provision for conferring benefits on persons of one sex only (disregarding any benefits to persons of the opposite sex which are exceptional or are relatively insignificant), being a provision which is contained in a charitable instrument.

(3) In the application of this section to England and Wales—
   (a) "charitable instrument" means an enactment or other instrument passed or made for charitable purposes, or an enactment or other instrument so far as it relates to charitable purposes;
   (b) "charitable purposes" means purposes which are exclusively charitable according to the law of England and Wales.

(4) In the application of this section to Scotland "charitable instrument" means an enactment or instrument passed or made by or on behalf of a body of persons or trust established for charitable purposes only.

PART V
Sport etc.

44. Nothing in Parts II to IV shall, in relation to any sport, game or other activity of a competitive nature where the physical strength, stamina or physique of the average woman puts her at a disadvantage to the average man, render unlawful any act related to the participation of a person as a competitor in events involving that activity which are confined to competitors of one sex.

Insurance etc.

45. Nothing in Parts II to IV shall render unlawful the treatment of a person in relation to an annuity, life assurance policy, accident insurance policy, or similar matter involving the assessment of risk, where the treatment—

(a) was effected by reference to actuarial or other data from a source on which it was reasonable to rely, and

(b) was reasonable having regard to the data and any other relevant factors.

Communal accommodation.

46.—(1) In this section "communal accommodation" means residential accommodation which includes dormitories or other shared sleeping accommodation which for reasons of privacy or decency should be used by men only, or by women only (but which may include some shared sleeping accommodation for men, and some for women, or some ordinary sleeping accommodation).

(2) In this section "communal accommodation" also includes residential accommodation all or part of which should be used by men only, or by women only, because of the nature of the sanitary facilities serving the accommodation.

(3) Nothing in Part II or III shall render unlawful sex discrimination in the admission of persons to communal accommodation if the accommodation is managed in a way which, given the exigencies of the situation, comes as near as may be to fair and equitable treatment of men and women.

(4) In applying subsection (3) account shall be taken of—

(a) whether and how far it is reasonable to expect that the accommodation should be altered or extended, or that further alternative accommodation should be provided; and

(b) the frequency of the demand or need for use of the accommodation by men as compared with women.

(5) Nothing in Part II or III shall render unlawful sex discrimination against a woman, or against a man, as respects the provision of any benefit, facility or service if—

(a) the benefit, facility or service cannot properly and effectively be provided except for those using communal accommodation, and

(b) in the relevant circumstances the woman or, as the case may be, the man could lawfully be refused the use of the accommodation by virtue of subsection (3).

PART V

(6) Neither subsection (3) nor subsection (5) is a defence to an act of sex discrimination under Part II unless such arrangements as are reasonably practicable are made to compensate for the detriment caused by the discrimination; but in considering under subsection (5)(b) whether the use of communal accommodation could lawfully be refused (in a case based on Part II), it shall be assumed that the requirements of this subsection have been complied with as respects subsection (3).

(7) Section 25 shall not apply to sex discrimination within subsection (3) or (5).

(8) This section is without prejudice to the generality of section 35(1)(c).

47.—(1) Nothing in Parts II to IV shall render unlawful any act done in relation to particular work by a training body in, or in connection with—

Discriminatory training by certain bodies.

 (a) affording women only, or men only, access to facilities for training which would help to fit them for that work, or

 (b) encouraging women only, or men only, to take advantage of opportunities for doing that work,

where it appears to the training body that at any time within the 12 months immediately preceding the doing of the act there were no persons of the sex in question doing that work in Great Britain, or the number of persons of that sex doing the work in Great Britain was comparatively small.

(2) Where in relation to particular work it appears to a training body that although the condition for the operation of subsection (1) is not met for the whole of Great Britain it is met for an area within Great Britain, nothing in Parts II to IV shall render unlawful any act done by the training body in, or in connection with—

 (a) affording persons who are of the sex in question, and who appear likely to take up that work in that area, access to facilities for training which would help to fit them for that work, or

 (b) encouraging persons of that sex to take advantage of opportunities in the area for doing that work.

(3) Nothing in Parts II to IV shall render unlawful any act done by a training body in, or in connection with, affording persons access to facilities for training which would help to fit

PART V them for employment, where it appears to the training body that those persons are in special need of training by reason of the period for which they have been discharging domestic or family responsibilities to the exclusion of regular full time employment.

The discrimination in relation to which this subsection applies may result from confining the training to persons who have been discharging domestic or family responsibilities, or from the way persons are selected for training, or both.

(4) In this section " training body " means—
    (a) a person mentioned in section 14(2)(a) or (b), or
    (b) any other person being a person designated for the purposes of this section in an order made by or on behalf of the Secretary of State,

and a person may be designated under paragraph (b) for the purposes of subsections (1) and (2) only, or of subsection (3) only, or for all those subsections.

Other discriminatory training etc.

48.—(1) Nothing in Parts II to IV shall render unlawful any act done by an employer in relation to particular work in his employment, being an act done in, or in connection with,—
    (a) affording his female employees only, or his male employees only, access to facilities for training which would help to fit them for that work, or
    (b) encouraging women only, or men only, to take advantage of opportunities for doing that work,

where at any time within the twelve months immediately preceding the doing of the act there were no persons of the sex in question among those doing that work or the number of persons of that sex doing the work was comparatively small.

(2) Nothing in section 12 shall render unlawful any act done by an organisation to which that section applies in, or in connection with,—
    (a) affording female members of the organisation only, or male members of the organisation only, access to facilities for training which would help to fit them for holding a post of any kind in the organisation, or
    (b) encouraging female members only, or male members only, to take advantage of opportunities for holding such posts in the organisation,

where at any time within the twelve months immediately preceding the doing of the act there were no persons of the sex in question among persons holding such posts in the organisation or the number of persons of that sex holding such posts was comparatively small.

(3) Nothing in Parts II to IV shall render unlawful any act done by an organisation to which section 12 applies in, or in connection with, encouraging women only, or men only, to become members of the organisation where at any time within the twelve months immediately preceding the doing of the act there were no persons of the sex in question among those members or the number of persons of that sex among the members was comparatively small.

49.—(1) If an organisation to which section 12 applies comprises a body the membership of which is wholly or mainly elected, nothing in section 12 shall render unlawful provision which ensures that a minimum number of persons of one sex are members of the body— Trade unions etc.: elective bodies.

(a) by reserving seats on the body for persons of that sex, or

(b) by making extra seats on the body available (by election or co-option or otherwise) for persons of that sex on occasions when the number of persons of that sex in the other seats is below the minimum,

where in the opinion of the organisation the provision is in the circumstances needed to secure a reasonable lower limit to the number of members of that sex serving on the body; and nothing in Parts II to IV shall render unlawful any act done in order to give effect to such a provision.

(2) This section shall not be taken as making lawful—

(a) discrimination in the arrangements for determining the persons entitled to vote in an election of members of the body, or otherwise to choose the persons to serve on the body, or

(b) discrimination in any arrangements concerning membership of the organisation itself.

50.—(1) References in this Act to the affording by any person of access to benefits, facilities or services are not limited to benefits, facilities or services provided by that person himself, but include any means by which it is in that person's power to facilitate access to benefits, facilities or services provided by any other person (the " actual provider "). Indirect access to benefits etc.

(2) Where by any provision of this Act the affording by any person of access to benefits, facilities or services in a discriminatory way is in certain circumstances prevented from being unlawful, the effect of the provision shall extend also to the liability under this Act of any actual provider.

PART V
Acts done under statutory authority.

51.—(1) Nothing in Parts II to IV shall render unlawful any act done by a person if it was necessary for him to do it in order to comply with a requirement—

(a) of an Act passed before this Act; or

(b) of an instrument made or approved (whether before or after the passing of this Act) by or under an Act passed before this Act.

(2) Where an Act passed after this Act re-enacts (with or without modification) a provision of an Act passed before this Act, subsection (1) shall apply to that provision as re-enacted as if it continued to be contained in an Act passed before this Act.

Acts safeguarding national security.

52.—(1) Nothing in Parts II to IV shall render unlawful an act done for the purpose of safeguarding national security.

(2) A certificate purporting to be signed by or on behalf of a Minister of the Crown and certifying that an act specified in the certificate was done for the purpose of safeguarding national security shall be conclusive evidence that it was done for that purpose.

(3) A document purporting to be a certificate such as is mentioned in subsection (2) shall be received in evidence and, unless the contrary is proved, shall be deemed to be such a certificate.

PART VI

EQUAL OPPORTUNITIES COMMISSION

Establishment and duties of Commission.

53.—(1) There shall be a body of Commissioners named the Equal Opportunities Commission, consisting of at least eight but not more than fifteen individuals each appointed by the Secretary of State on a full-time or part-time basis, which shall have the following duties—

(a) to work towards the elimination of discrimination,

(b) to promote equality of opportunity between men and women generally, and

1970 c. 41.

(c) to keep under review the working of this Act and the Equal Pay Act 1970 and, when they are so required by the Secretary of State or otherwise think it necessary, draw up and submit to the Secretary of State proposals for amending them.

(2) The Secretary of State shall appoint—

(a) one of the Commissioners to be chairman of the Commission, and

(b) either one or two of the Commissioners (as the Secretary of State thinks fit) to be deputy chairman or deputy chairmen of the Commission.

PART V

(3) The Secretary of State may by order amend subsection (1) so far as it regulates the number of Commissioners.

(4) Schedule 3 shall have effect with respect to the Commission.

54.—(1) The Commission may undertake or assist (financially or otherwise) the undertaking by other persons of any research, and any educational activities, which appear to the Commission necessary or expedient for the purposes of section 53(1).

Research and education.

(2) The Commission may make charges for educational or other facilities or services made available by them.

55.—(1) Without prejudice to the generality of section 53(1), the Commission, in pursuance of the duties imposed by paragraphs (a) and (b) of that subsection—

Review of discriminatory provisions in health and safety legislation.

(a) shall keep under review the relevant statutory provisions in so far as they require men and women to be treated differently, and

(b) if so required by the Secretary of State, make to him a report on any matter specified by him which is connected with those duties and concerns the relevant statutory provisions.

Any such report shall be made within the time specified by the Secretary of State, and the Secretary of State shall cause the report to be published.

(2) Whenever the Commission think it necessary, they shall draw up and submit to the Secretary of State proposals for amending the relevant statutory provisions.

(3) The Commission shall carry out their duties in relation to the relevant statutory provisions in consultation with the Health and Safety Commission.

(4) In this section " the relevant statutory provisions " has the meaning given by section 53 of the Health and Safety at Work etc. Act 1974.

1974 c. 37.

56.—(1) As soon as practicable after the end of each calendar year the Commission shall make to the Secretary of State a report on their activities during the year (an " annual report ").

Annual reports.

(2) Each annual report shall include a general survey of developments, during the period to which it relates, in respect of matters falling within the scope of the Commission's duties.

PART VI

(3) The Secretary of State shall lay a copy of every annual report before each House of Parliament, and shall cause the report to be published.

Investigations

Power to conduct formal investigations.

57.—(1) Without prejudice to their general power to do anything requisite for the performance of their duties under section 53(1), the Commission may if they think fit, and shall if required by the Secretary of State, conduct a formal investigation for any purpose connected with the carrying out of those duties.

(2) The Commission may, with the approval of the Secretary of State, appoint, on a full-time or part-time basis, one or more individuals as additional Commissioners for the purposes of a formal investigation.

(3) The Commission may nominate one or more Commissioners, with or without one or more additional Commissioners, to conduct a formal investigation on their behalf, and may delegate any of their functions in relation to the investigation to the persons so nominated.

Terms of reference.

58.—(1) The Commission shall not embark on a formal investigation unless the requirements of this section have been complied with.

(2) Terms of reference for the investigation shall be drawn up by the Commission or, if the Commission were required by the Secretary of State to conduct the investigation, by the Secretary of State after consulting the Commission.

(3) It shall be the duty of the Commission to give general notice of the holding of the investigation unless the terms of reference confine it to activities of persons named in them, but in such a case the Commission shall in the prescribed manner give those persons notice of the holding of the investigation.

(4) The Commission or, if the Commission were required by the Secretary of State to conduct the investigation, the Secretary of State after consulting the Commission may from time to time revise the terms of reference; and subsections (1) and (3) shall apply to the revised investigation and terms of reference as they applied to the original.

Power to obtain information.

59.—(1) For the purposes of a formal investigation the Commission, by a notice in the prescribed form served on him in the prescribed manner,—

(*a*) may require any person to furnish such written information as may be described in the notice, and may specify the time at which, and the manner and form in which, the information is to be furnished;

(b) may require any person to attend at such time and place as is specified in the notice and give oral information about, and produce all documents in his possession or control relating to, any matter specified in the notice.

(2) Except as provided by section 69, a notice shall be served under subsection (1) only where—
  (a) service of the notice was authorised by an order made by or on behalf of the Secretary of State, or
  (b) the terms of reference of the investigation state that the Commission believe that a person named in them may have done or may be doing acts of all or any of the following descriptions—
    (i) unlawful discriminatory acts,
    (ii) contraventions of section 37,
    (iii) contraventions of sections 38, 39 or 40, and
    (iv) acts in breach of a term modified or included by virtue of an equality clause,
  and confine the investigation to those acts.

(3) A notice under subsection (1) shall not require a person—
  (a) to give information, or produce any documents, which he could not be compelled to give in evidence, or produce, in civil proceedings before the High Court or the Court of Session, or
  (b) to attend at any place unless the necessary expenses of his journey to and from that place are paid or tendered to him.

(4) If a person fails to comply with a notice served on him under subsection (1) or the Commission has reasonable cause to believe that he intends not to comply with it, the Commission may apply to a county court for an order requiring him to comply with it or with such directions for the like purpose as may be contained in the order; and section 84 (penalty for neglecting witness summons) of the County Courts Act 1959 shall apply to failure without reasonable excuse to comply with any such order as it applies in the cases there provided.

(5) In the application of subsection (4) to Scotland—
  (a) for the reference to a county court there shall be substituted a reference to a sheriff court, and
  (b) for the words after " order; and " to the end of the subsection there shall be substituted the words " paragraph 73 of the First Schedule to the Sheriff Courts (Scotland) Act 1907 (power of sheriff to grant second diligence for

PART VI

compelling the attendances of witnesses or havers) shall apply to any such order as it applies in proceedings in the sheriff court ".

(6) A person commits an offence if he—

(a) wilfully alters, suppresses, conceals or destroys a document which he has been required by a notice or order under this section to produce, or

(b) in complying with such a notice or order, knowingly or recklessly makes any statement which is false in a material particular,

and shall be liable on summary conviction to a fine not exceeding £400.

(7) Proceedings for an offence under subsection (6) may (without prejudice to any jurisdiction exercisable apart from this subsection) be instituted—

(a) against any person at any place at which he has an office or other place of business;

(b) against an individual at any place where he resides, or at which he is for the time being.

Recommendations and reports on formal investigations.

60.—(1) If in the light of any of their findings in a formal investigation it appears to the Commission necessary or expedient, whether during the course of the investigation or after its conclusion,—

(a) to make to any persons, with a view to promoting equality of opportunity between men and women who are affected by any of their activities, recommendations for changes in their policies or procedures, or as to any other matters, or

(b) to make to the Secretary of State any recommendations, whether for changes in the law or otherwise,

the Commission shall make those recommendations accordingly.

(2) The Commission shall prepare a report of their findings in any formal investigation conducted by them.

(3) If the formal investigation is one required by the Secretary of State—

(a) the Commission shall deliver the report to the Secretary of State, and

(b) the Secretary of State shall cause the report to be published,

and unless required by the Secretary of State the Commission shall not publish the report.

(4) If the formal investigation is not one required by the Secretary of State, the Commission shall either publish the report, or make it available for inspection in accordance with subsection (5).

(5) Where under subsection (4) a report is to be made available for inspection, any person shall be entitled, on payment of such fee (if any) as may be determined by the Commission—
- (a) to inspect the report during ordinary office hours and take copies of all or any part of the report, or
- (b) to obtain from the Commission a copy, certified by the Commission to be correct, of the report.

(6) The Commission may if they think fit determine that the right conferred by subsection (5)(a) shall be exercisable in relation to a copy of the report instead of, or in addition to, the original.

(7) The Commission shall give general notice of the place or places where, and the times when, reports may be inspected under subsection (5).

61.—(1) No information given to the Commission by any person ("the informant") in connection with a formal investigation shall be disclosed by the Commission, or by any person who is or has been a Commissioner, additional Commissioner or employee of the Commission, except—

Restriction on disclosure of information.

- (a) on the order of any court, or
- (b) with the informant's consent, or
- (c) in the form of a summary or other general statement published by the Commission which does not identify the informant or any other person to whom the information relates, or
- (d) in a report of the investigation published by the Commission or made available for inspection under section 60(5), or
- (e) to the Commissioners, additional Commissioners or employees of the Commission, or, so far as may be necessary for the proper performance of the functions of the Commission, to other persons, or
- (f) for the purpose of any civil proceedings under this Act to which the Commission are a party, or any criminal proceedings.

(2) Any person who discloses information in contravention of subsection (1) commits an offence and shall be liable on summary conviction to a fine not exceeding £400.

PART VI

(3) In preparing any report for publication or for inspection the Commission shall exclude, so far as is consistent with their duties and the object of the report, any matter which relates to the private affairs of any individual or business interests of any person where the publication of that matter might, in the opinion of the Commission, prejudicially affect that individual or person.

PART VII

ENFORCEMENT

General

No further sanctions for breach of Act.
62.—(1) A contravention of this Act shall incur as such no sanction, whether civil or criminal, except to the extent (if any) expressly provided by this Act.

(2) In subsection (1) " sanction " includes the granting of an injunction or declaration, but does not include the making of an order of certiorari, mandamus or prohibition.

(3) Subsection (2) does not affect the remedies available under section 66(2), notwithstanding that subsection (2) would prevent those remedies being obtainable in the High Court.

(4) In relation to Scotland in subsection (1) " sanction " includes the granting of an interdict or of a declarator or a decree ad factum praestandum, but otherwise nothing in this Act shall affect any right to bring any proceedings, whether civil or criminal, which might have been brought if this Act had not been passed.

Enforcement in employment field

Jurisdiction of industrial tribunals.
63.—(1) A complaint by any person (" the complainant ") that another person (" the respondent ")—

(*a*) has committed an act of discrimination against the complainant which is unlawful by virtue of Part II, or

(*b*) is by virtue of section 41 or 42 to be treated as having committed such an act of discrimination against the complainant,

may be presented to an industrial tribunal.

(2) Subsection (1) does not apply to a complaint under section 13(1) of an act in respect of which an appeal, or proceedings in the nature of an appeal, may be brought under any enactment.

Conciliation in employment cases.
1970 c. 41.
64.—(1) Where a complaint has been presented to an industrial tribunal under section 63, or under section 2(1) of the Equal Pay Act 1970, and a copy of the complaint has been sent to a conciliation officer, it shall be the duty of the conciliation officer—

(a) if he is requested to do so both by the complainant and the respondent, or
(b) if, in the absence of requests by the complainant and the respondent, he considers that he could act under this subsection with a reasonable prospect of success,

to endeavour to promote a settlement of the complaint without its being determined by an industrial tribunal.

(2) Where, before a complaint such as is mentioned in subsection (1) has been presented to an industrial tribunal, a request is made to a conciliation officer to make his services available in the matter by a person who, if the complaint were so presented, would be the complainant or respondent, subsection (1) shall apply as if the complaint had been so presented and a copy of it had been sent to the conciliation officer.

(3) In proceeding under subsection (1) or (2), a conciliation officer shall where appropriate have regard to the desirability of encouraging the use of other procedures available for the settlement of grievances.

(4) Anything communicated to a conciliation officer in connection with the performance of his functions under this section shall not be admissible in evidence in any proceedings before an industrial tribunal except with the consent of the person who communicated it to that officer.

65.—(1) Where an industrial tribunal finds that a complaint presented to it under section 63 is well-founded the tribunal shall make such of the following as it considers just and equitable—

(a) an order declaring the rights of the complainant and the respondent in relation to the act to which the complaint relates;
(b) an order requiring the respondent to pay to the complainant compensation of an amount corresponding to any damages he could have been ordered by a county court or by a sheriff court to pay to the complainant if the complaint had fallen to be dealt with under section 66;
(c) a recommendation that the respondent take within a specified period action appearing to the tribunal to be practicable for the purpose of obviating or reducing the adverse effect on the complainant of any act of discrimination to which the complaint relates.

(2) The amount of compensation awarded to a person under subsection (1)(b) shall not exceed the amount for the time being specified in paragraph 20(1)(b) of Schedule 1 to the Trade Union and Labour Relations Act 1974.

PART VII

(3) If without reasonable justification the respondent to a complaint fails to comply with a recommendation made by an industrial tribunal under subsection (1)(c), then, if they think it just and equitable to do so—

(a) the tribunal may increase the amount of compensation required to be paid to the complainant in respect of the complaint by an order made under subsection (1)(b), or

(b) if an order under subsection (1)(b) could have been made but was not, the tribunal may make such an order.

Enforcement of Part III

Claims under Part III.

66.—(1) A claim by any person (" the claimant ") that another person (" the respondent ")—

(a) has committed an act of discrimination against the claimant which is unlawful by virtue of Part III, or

(b) is by virtue of section 41 or 42 to be treated as having committed such an act of discrimination against the claimant,

may be made the subject of civil proceedings in like manner as any other claim in tort or (in Scotland) in reparation for breach of statutory duty.

(2) Proceedings under subsection (1)—

(a) shall be brought in England and Wales only in a county court, and

(b) shall be brought in Scotland only in a sheriff court,

but all such remedies shall be obtainable in such proceedings as, apart from this subsection, would be obtainable in the High Court or the Court of Session, as the case may be.

(3) As respects an unlawful act of discrimination falling within section 1(1)(b) (or, where this section is applied by section 65(1)(b), section 3(1)(b)) no award of damages shall be made if the respondent proves that the requirement or condition in question was not applied with the intention of treating the claimant unfavourably on the ground of his sex or marital status as the case may be.

(4) For the avoidance of doubt it is hereby declared that damages in respect of an unlawful act of discrimination may include compensation for injury to feelings whether or not they include compensation under any other head.

(5) Civil proceedings in respect of a claim by any person that he has been discriminated against in contravention of section 22 or 23 by a body to which section 25(1) applies shall not be

instituted unless the claimant has given notice of the claim to the Secretary of State and either the Secretary of State has by notice informed the claimant that the Secretary of State does not require further time to consider the matter, or the period of two months has elapsed since the claimant gave notice to the Secretary of State; but nothing in this subsection applies to a counterclaim.

PART VII

(6) For the purposes of proceedings under subsection (1)—
  (a) section 91(1) (power of judge to appoint assessors) of the County Courts Act 1959 shall apply with the omission of the words " on the application of any party ", and

1959 c. 22.

  (b) the remuneration of assessors appointed under the said section 91(1) shall be at such rate as may be determined by the Lord Chancellor with the approval of the Minister for the Civil Service.

(7) For the purpose of proceedings before the sheriff, provision may be made by act of sederunt for the appointment of assessors by him, and the remuneration of any assessors so appointed shall be at such rate as the Lord President of the Court of Session with the approval of the Minister for the Civil Service may determine.

(8) A county court or sheriff court shall have jurisdiction to entertain proceedings under subsection (1) with respect to an act done on a ship, aircraft or hovercraft outside its district, including such an act done outside Great Britain.

Non-discrimination notices

67.—(1) This section applies to—
  (a) an unlawful discriminatory act, and
  (b) a contravention of section 37, and
  (c) a contravention of section 38, 39 or 40, and
  (d) an act in breach of a term modified or included by virtue of an equality clause,
and so applies whether or not proceedings have been brought in respect of the act.

Issue of non-discrimination notice.

(2) If in the course of a formal investigation the Commission become satisfied that a person is committing, or has committed, any such acts, the Commission may in the prescribed manner serve on him a notice in the prescribed form (" a non-discrimination notice ") requiring him—
  (a) not to commit any such acts, and

(b) where compliance with paragraph (a) involves changes in any of his practices or other arrangements—

(i) to inform the Commission that he has effected those changes and what those changes are, and

(ii) to take such steps as may be reasonably required by the notice for the purpose of affording that information to other persons concerned.

(3) A non-discrimination notice may also require the person on whom it is served to furnish the Commission with such other information as may be reasonably required by the notice in order to verify that the notice has been complied with.

(4) The notice may specify the time at which, and the manner and form in which, any information is to be furnished to the Commission, but the time at which any information is to be furnished in compliance with the notice shall not be later than five years after the notice has become final.

(5) The Commission shall not serve a non-discrimination notice in respect of any person unless they have first—

(a) given him notice that they are minded to issue a non-discrimination notice in his case, specifying the grounds on which they contemplate doing so, and

(b) offered him an opportunity of making oral or written representations in the matter (or both oral and written representations if he thinks fit) within a period of not less than 28 days specified in the notice, and

(c) taken account of any representations so made by him.

(6) Subsection (2) does not apply to any acts in respect of which the Secretary of State could exercise the powers conferred on him by section 25(2) and (3); but if the Commission become aware of any such acts they shall give notice of them to the Secretary of State.

(7) Section 59(4) shall apply to requirements under subsection (2)(b), (3) and (4) contained in a non-discrimination notice which has become final as it applies to requirements in a notice served under section 59 (1).

Appeal against non-discrimination notice.

68.—(1) Not later than six weeks after a non-discrimination notice is served on any person he may appeal against any requirement of the notice—

(a) to an industrial tribunal, so far as the requirement relates to acts which are within the jurisdiction of the tribunal;

(b) to a county court or to a sheriff court so far as the requirement relates to acts which are within the jurisdiction of the court and are not within the jurisdiction of an industrial tribunal.

(2) Where the court or tribunal considers a requirement in respect of which an appeal is brought under subsection (1) to be unreasonable because it is based on an incorrect finding of fact or for any other reason, the court or tribunal shall quash the requirement.

(3) On quashing a requirement under subsection (2) the court or tribunal may direct that the non-discrimination notice shall be treated as if, in place of the requirement quashed, it had contained a requirement in terms specified in the direction.

(4) Subsection (1) does not apply to a requirement treated as included in a non-discrimination notice by virtue of a direction under subsection (3).

69.—(1) If—

(a) the terms of reference of a formal investigation state that its purpose is to determine whether any requirements of a non-discrimination notice are being or have been carried out, but section 59(2)(b) does not apply, and

(b) section 58(3) is complied with in relation to the investigation on a date ("the commencement date") not later than the expiration of the period of five years beginning when the non-discrimination notice became final,

the Commission may within the period referred to in subsection (2) serve notices under section 59(1) for the purposes of the investigation without needing to obtain the consent of the Secretary of State.

Investigation as to compliance with non-discrimination notice.

(2) The said period begins on the commencement date and ends on the later of the following dates

(a) the date on which the period of five years mentioned in subsection (1)(b) expires;

(b) the date two years after the commencement date.

70.—(1) The Commission shall establish and maintain a register ("the register") of non-discrimination notices which have become final.

Register of non-discrimination notices.

(2) Any person shall be entitled, on payment of such fee (if any) as may be determined by the Commission,—

(a) to inspect the register during ordinary office hours and take copies of any entry, or

PART VII

(b) to obtain from the Commission a copy, certified by the Commission to be correct, of any entry in the register.

(3) The Commission may, if they think fit, determine that the right conferred by subsection (2)(a) shall be exercisable in relation to a copy of the register instead of, or in addition to, the original.

(4) The Commission shall give general notice of the place or places where, and the times when, the register or a copy of it may be inspected.

Other enforcement by Commission

Persistent discrimination.

71.—(1) If, during the period of five years beginning on the date on which either of the following became final in the case of any person, namely,—

    (a) a non-discrimination notice served on him,

1970 c. 41.

    (b) a finding by a court or tribunal under section 63 or 66, or section 2 of the Equal Pay Act 1970, that he has done an unlawful discriminatory act or an act in breach of a term modified or included by virtue of an equality clause,

it appears to the Commission that unless restrained he is likely to do one or more acts falling within paragraph (b), or contravening section 37, the Commission may apply to a county court for an injunction, or to the sheriff court for an order, restraining him from doing so; and the court, if satisfied that the application is well-founded, may grant the injunction or order in the terms applied for or in more limited terms.

(2) In proceedings under this section the Commission shall not allege that the person to whom the proceedings relate has done an act which is within the jurisdiction of an industrial tribunal unless a finding by an industrial tribunal that he did that act has become final.

Enforcement of ss. 38 to 40.

72.—(1) Proceedings in respect of a contravention of section 38, 39 or 40 shall be brought only by the Commission in accordance with the following provisions of this section.

(2) The proceedings shall be—

    (a) an application for a decision whether the alleged contravention occurred, or

    (b) an application under subsection (4) below,

or both.

(3) An application under subsection (2)(*a*) shall be made—

    (*a*) in a case based on any provision of Part II, to an industrial tribunal, and

    (*b*) in any other case to a county court or sheriff court.

(4) If it appears to the Commission—

    (*a*) that a person has done an act which by virtue of section 38, 39 or 40 was unlawful, and

    (*b*) that unless restrained he is likely to do further acts which by virtue of that section are unlawful,

the Commission may apply to a county court for an injunction, or to a sheriff court for an order, restraining him from doing such acts; and the court, if satisfied that the application is well-founded, may grant the injunction or an order in the terms applied for or more limited terms.

(5) In proceedings under subsection (4) the Commission shall not allege that the person to whom the proceedings relate has done an act which is unlawful under this Act and within the jurisdiction of an industrial tribunal unless a finding by an industrial tribunal that he did that act has become final.

73.—(1) With a view to making an application under section 71(1) or 72(4) in relation to a person the Commission may present to an industrial tribunal a complaint that he has done an act within the jurisdiction of an industrial tribunal, and if the tribunal considers that the complaint is well-founded they shall make a finding to that effect and, if they think it just and equitable to do so in the case of an act contravening any provision of Part II may also (as if the complaint had been presented by the person discriminated against) make an order such as is referred to in section 65(1)(*a*), or a recommendation such as is referred to in section 65(1)(*c*), or both.

Preliminary action in employment cases.

(2) Subsection (1) is without prejudice to the jurisdiction conferred by section 72(2).

(3) Any finding of an industrial tribunal under—

    (*a*) this Act, or

    (*b*) the Equal Pay Act 1970,

1970 c. 41.

in respect of any act shall, if it has become final, be treated as conclusive—

    (i) by the county court or sheriff court on an application under section 71(1) or 72(4) or in proceedings on an equality clause,

    (ii) by an industrial tribunal on a complaint made by the person affected by the act under section 63 or in relation to an equality clause.

PART VII

1970 c. 41.

(4) In sections 71 and 72 and this section, the acts "within the jurisdiction of an industrial tribunal" are those in respect of which such jurisdiction is conferred by sections 63 and 72 and by section 2 of the Equal Pay Act 1970.

Help for persons suffering discrimination

Help for aggrieved persons in obtaining information etc.

74.—(1) With a view to helping a person ("the person aggrieved") who considers he may have been discriminated against in contravention of this Act to decide whether to institute proceedings and, if he does so, to formulate and present his case in the most effective manner, the Secretary of State shall by order prescribe—

  (a) forms by which the person aggrieved may question the respondent on his reasons for doing any relevant act, or on any other matter which is or may be relevant;

  (b) forms by which the respondent may if he so wishes reply to any questions.

(2) Where the person aggrieved questions the respondent (whether in accordance with an order under subsection (1) or not)—

  (a) the question, and any reply by the respondent (whether in accordance with such an order or not) shall, subject to the following provisions of this section, be admissible as evidence in the proceedings;

  (b) if it appears to the court or tribunal that the respondent deliberately, and without reasonable excuse, omitted to reply within a reasonable period or that his reply is evasive or equivocal, the court or tribunal may draw any inference from that fact that it considers it just and equitable to draw, including an inference that he committed an unlawful act.

(3) The Secretary of State may by order—

  (a) prescribe the period within which questions must be duly served in order to be admissible under subsection (2)(a), and

  (b) prescribe the manner in which a question, and any reply by the respondent, may be duly served.

(4) Rules may enable the court entertaining a claim under section 66 to determine, before the date fixed for the hearing of the claim, whether a question or reply is admissible under this section or not.

(5) This section is without prejudice to any other enactment or rule of law regulating interlocutory and preliminary matters in proceedings before a county court, sheriff court or industrial

tribunal, and has effect subject to any enactment or rule of law regulating the admissibility of evidence in such proceedings.

(6) In this section "respondent" includes a prospective respondent and "rules"—

(a) in relation to county court proceedings, means county court rules;

(b) in relation to sheriff court proceedings, means sheriff court rules.

75.—(1) Where, in relation to proceedings or prospective proceedings either under this Act or in respect of an equality clause, an individual who is an actual or prospective complainant or claimant applies to the Commission for assistance under this section, the Commission shall consider the application and may grant it if they think fit to do so on the ground that—

Assistance by Commission.

(a) the case raises a question of principle, or

(b) it is unreasonable, having regard to the complexity of the case or the applicant's position in relation to the respondent or another person involved or any other matter, to expect the applicant to deal with the case unaided,

or by reason of any other special consideration.

(2) Assistance by the Commission under this section may include—

(a) giving advice;

(b) procuring or attempting to procure the settlement of any matter in dispute;

(c) arranging for the giving of advice or assistance by a solicitor or counsel;

(d) arranging for representation by any person including all such assistance as is usually given by a solicitor or counsel in the steps preliminary or incidental to any proceedings, or in arriving at or giving effect to a compromise to avoid or bring to an end any proceedings,

but paragraph (d) shall not affect the law and practice regulating the descriptions of persons who may appear in, conduct, defend and address the court in, any proceedings.

(3) In so far as expenses are incurred by the Commission in providing the applicant with assistance under this section the recovery of those expenses (as taxed or assessed in such manner as may be prescribed by rules or regulations) shall constitute a first charge for the benefit of the Commission—

(a) on any costs or expenses which (whether by virtue of a

judgment or order of a court or tribunal or an agreement or otherwise) are payable to the applicant by any other person in respect of the matter in connection with which the assistance is given, and

(b) so far as relates to any costs or expenses, on his rights under any compromise or settlement arrived at in connection with that matter to avoid or bring to an end any proceedings.

(4) The charge conferred by subsection (3) is subject to any charge under the Legal Aid Act 1974, or any charge or obligation for payment in priority to other debts under the Legal Aid and Advice (Scotland) Acts 1967 and 1972, and is subject to any provision in any of those Acts for payment of any sum into the legal aid fund.

(5) In this section "respondent" includes a prospective respondent and "rules or regulations"—

(a) in relation to county court proceedings, means county court rules;
(b) in relation to sheriff court proceedings, means sheriff court rules;
(c) in relation to industrial tribunal proceedings, means regulations made under paragraph 21 of Schedule 1 to the Trade Union and Labour Relations Act 1974.

Period within which proceedings to be brought

76.—(1) An industrial tribunal shall not consider a complaint under section 63 unless it is presented to the tribunal before the end of the period of three months beginning when the act complained of was done.

(2) A county court or a sheriff court shall not consider a claim under section 66 unless proceedings in respect of the claim are instituted before the end of the period of six months beginning—

(a) when the act complained of was done, or
(b) in a case to which section 66(5) applies, when the restriction on the institution of proceedings imposed by that provision ceased to operate.

(3) A county court or sheriff court shall not consider an application under section 72 unless it is made before the end of the period of six months beginning when the act to which it relates was done.

(4) An industrial tribunal shall not consider a complaint under section 73(1) unless it is presented to the tribunal before the end of the period of six months beginning when the act complained of was done.

(5) A court or tribunal may nevertheless consider any such complaint, claim or application which is out of time if, in all the circumstances of the case, it considers that it is just and equitable to do so.

(6) For the purposes of this section—
- (a) where the inclusion of any term in a contract renders the making of the contract an unlawful act that act shall be treated as extending throughout the duration of the contract, and
- (b) any act extending over a period shall be treated as done at the end of that period, and
- (c) a deliberate omission shall be treated as done when the person in question decided upon it,

and in the absence of evidence establishing the contrary a person shall be taken for the purposes of this section to decide upon an omission when he does an act inconsistent with doing the omitted act or, if he has done no such inconsistent act, when the period expires within which he might reasonably have been expected to do the omitted act if it was to be done.

PART VIII

SUPPLEMENTAL

77.—(1) A term of a contract is void where— *Validity and revision of contracts.*
- (a) its inclusion renders the making of the contract unlawful by virtue of this Act, or
- (b) it is included in furtherance of an act rendered unlawful by this Act, or
- (c) it provides for the doing of an act which would be rendered unlawful by this Act.

(2) Subsection (1) does not apply to a term the inclusion of which constitutes, or is in furtherance of, or provides for, unlawful discrimination against a party to the contract, but the term shall be unenforceable against that party.

(3) A term in a contract which purports to exclude or limit any provision of this Act or the Equal Pay Act 1970 is unenforceable by any person in whose favour the term would operate apart from this subsection. 1970 c. 41.

(4) Subsection (3) does not apply—
- (a) to a contract settling a complaint to which section 63(1) of this Act or section 2 of the Equal Pay Act 1970 applies where the contract is made with the assistance of a conciliation officer;
- (b) to a contract settling a claim to which section 66 applies.

PART VIII

(5) On the application of any person interested in a contract to which subsection (2) applies, a county court or sheriff court may make such order as it thinks just for removing or modifying any term made unenforceable by that subsection; but such an order shall not be made unless all persons affected have been given notice of the application (except where under rules of court notice may be dispensed with) and have been afforded an opportunity to make representations to the court.

(6) An order under subsection (5) may include provision as respects any period before the making of the order.

Educational charities in England and Wales.

78.—(1) This section applies to any trust deed or other instrument—

(a) which concerns property applicable for or in connection with the provision of education in any establishment in paragraphs 1 to 5 of the Table in section 22, and

(b) which in any way restricts the benefits available under the instrument to persons of one sex.

(2) If on the application of the trustees, or of the responsible body (as defined in section 22), the Secretary of State is satisfied that the removal or modification of the restriction would conduce to the advancement of education without sex discrimination, he may by order make such modifications of the instrument as appear to him expedient for removing or modifying the restriction, and for any supplemental or incidental purposes.

(3) If the trust was created by gift or bequest, no order shall be made until 25 years after the date on which the gift or bequest took effect, unless the donor or his personal representatives, or the personal representatives of the testator, have consented in writing to the making of the application for the order.

(4) The Secretary of State shall require the applicant to publish notice—

(a) containing particulars of the proposed order, and

(b) stating that representations may be made to the Secretary of State within a period specified in the notice.

(5) The period specified in the notice shall not be less than one month from the date of the notice.

(6) The applicants shall publish the notice in such manner as may be specified by the Secretary of State, and the cost of any publication of the notice may be defrayed out of the property of the trust.

(7) Before making the order the Secretary of State shall take into account any representations duly made in accordance with the notice.

(8) This section does not apply in Scotland.

79.—(1) This section applies to any educational endowment to which Part VI of the Education (Scotland) Act 1962 applies and which in any way restricts the benefit of the endowment to persons of one sex, and any reference to an educational endowment in this section includes a reference to—

    (a) a scheme made or approved for that endowment under that Part of the Education (Scotland) Act 1962;

    (b) any endowment which is, by virtue of section 121(1) of that Act, dealt with as if it were an educational endowment; and

    (c) a university endowment, the Carnegie Trust, a theological endowment and a new endowment.

(2) If, on the application of the governing body of an educational endowment, the Secretary of State is satisfied that the removal or modification of the provision which restricts the benefit of the endowment to persons of one sex would conduce to the advancement of education without sex discrimination, he may, by order, make such modifications to the endowment as appear to him expedient for removing or modifying the restriction and for any supplemental or incidental purposes.

(3) Where the Secretary of State proposes to make an order under this section, he shall publish a notice, in such manner as he thinks sufficient for giving information to persons whom he considers may be interested in the endowment—

    (a) containing particulars of the proposed order; and

    (b) stating that representations may be made with respect thereto within such period as may be specified in the notice, not being less than one month from the date of publication of the notice,

and the cost of publication of any such notice shall be paid out of the funds of the endowment to which the notice relates.

(4) Before making any order under this section, the Secretary of State shall consider any representations duly made in accordance with the said notice and he may cause a local inquiry to be held into such representations under section 68 of the Education (Scotland) Act 1962.

(5) Without prejudice to section 81(5) of this Act, any order made under this section may be varied or revoked in a scheme made or approved under Part VI of the Education (Scotland) Act 1962.

PART VIII
1962 c. 47.

(6) For paragraph (*b*) of section 123(1) of the Education (Scotland) Act 1962, there shall be substituted the following paragraph—

"(*b*) where he considers it expedient to do so, provide for extending to both sexes the benefit of the endowment".

(7) This section shall be construed as one with Part VI of the Education (Scotland) Act 1962.

Power to amend certain provisions of Act.

80.—(1) The Secretary of State may by an order the draft of which has been approved by each House of Parliament—

(*a*) amend any of the following provisions, namely, sections 6(3), 7, 19, 20(1), (2) and (3), 31(2), 32, 34, 35 and 43 to 48 (including any such provision as amended by a previous order under this subsection);

(*b*) amend or repeal any of the following provisions, namely, sections 11(4), 12(4), 33 and 49 (including any such provision as amended by a previous order under this subsection);

(*c*) amend Part II, III or IV so as to render lawful an act which, apart from the amendment, would be unlawful by reason of section 6(1) or (2), 29(1), 30 or 31;

(*d*) amend section 11(1) so as to alter the number of partners specified in that provision.

(2) The Secretary of State shall not lay before Parliament the draft of an order under subsection (1) unless he has consulted the Commission about the contents of the draft.

(3) An order under subsection (1)(*c*) may make such amendments to the list of provisions given in subsection (1)(*a*) as in the opinion of the Secretary of State are expedient having regard to the contents of the order.

Orders.

81.—(1) Any power of the Secretary of State to make orders under the provisions of this Act (except sections 14(2)(*d*), 27, 47(4)(*b*) and 59(2)) shall be exercisable by statutory instrument.

(2) An order made by the Secretary of State under the preceding provisions of this Act (except sections 14(2)(*d*), 27, 47(4)(*b*), 59(2) and 80(1)) shall be subject to annulment in pursuance of a resolution of either House of Parliament.

(3) Subsections (1) and (2) do not apply to an order under section 78 or 79, but—

(*a*) an order under section 78 which modifies an enactment, and

(*b*) any order under section 79 other than one which relates to an endowment to which section 128 of the Education (Scotland) Act 1962 (small endowments) applies, shall be made by statutory instrument subject to annulment in pursuance of a resolution of either House of Parliament.

PART VIII

(4) An order under this Act may make different provision in relation to different cases or classes of case, may exclude certain cases or classes of case, and may contain transitional provisions and savings.

(5) Any power conferred by this Act to make orders includes power (exercisable in the like manner and subject to the like conditions) to vary or revoke any order so made.

82.—(1) In this Act, unless the context otherwise requires—

General interpretation provisions.

"access" shall be construed in accordance with section 50;

"act" includes a deliberate omission;

"advertisement" includes every form of advertisement, whether to the public or not, and whether in a newspaper or other publication, by television or radio, by display of notices, signs, labels, showcards or goods, by distribution of samples, circulars, catalogues, price lists or other material, by exhibition of pictures, models or films, or in any other way, and references to the publishing of advertisements shall be construed accordingly;

"associated employer" shall be construed in accordance with subsection (2);

"the Commission" means the Equal Opportunities Commission;

"Commissioner" means a member of the Commission;

"conciliation officer" means a person appointed under paragraph 26(1) of Schedule 1 to the Trade Union and Labour Relations Act 1974;

1974 c. 52.

"designate" shall be construed in accordance with subsection (3);

"discrimination" and related terms shall be construed in accordance with section 5(1);

"dispose", in relation to premises, includes granting a right to occupy the premises, and any reference to acquiring premises shall be construed accordingly;

"education" includes any form of training or instruction;

"education authority" and "educational establishment" in relation to Scotland have the same meaning as they have respectively in section 145(16) and (17) of the Education (Scotland) Act 1962

1962 c. 47.

PART VIII

"employment" means employment under a contract of service or of apprenticeship or a contract personally to execute any work or labour, and related expressions shall be construed accordingly;

"employment agency" means a person who, for profit or not, provides services for the purpose of finding employment for workers or supplying employers with workers;

1970 c. 41.
"equality clause" has the meaning given in section 1(2) of the Equal Pay Act 1970 (as set out in section 8(1) of this Act);

"estate agent" means a person who, by way of profession or trade, provides services for the purpose of finding premises for persons seeking to acquire them or assisting in the disposal of premises;

"final" shall be construed in accordance with subsection (4);

1890 c. 39.
"firm" has the meaning given by section 4 of the Partnership Act 1890;

"formal investigation" means an investigation under section 57;

1944 c. 31.
1962 c. 47.
"further education" has the meaning given by section 41(a) of the Education Act 1944 and in Scotland has the meaning given by section 145(21) of the Education (Scotland) Act 1962;

"general notice", in relation to any person, means a notice published by him at a time and in a manner appearing to him suitable for securing that the notice is seen within a reasonable time by persons likely to be affected by it;

"genuine occupational qualification" shall be construed in accordance with section 7(2);

"Great Britain" includes such of the territorial waters of the United Kingdom as are adjacent to Great Britain;

"independent school" has the meaning given by section 114(1) of the Education Act 1944 and in Scotland has the meaning given by section 145(23) of the Education (Scotland) Act 1962;

1964 c. 16.
"industrial tribunal" means a tribunal established under section 12 of the Industrial Training Act 1964;

"man" includes a male of any age;

"managers" has the same meaning for Scotland as in section 145(26) of the Education (Scotland) Act 1962;

"near relative" shall be construed in accordance with subsection (5);

PART VIII

"non-discrimination notice" means a notice under section 67;

"notice" means a notice in writing;

"prescribed" means prescribed by regulations made by the Secretary of State by statutory instrument;

"profession" includes any vocation or occupation;

"proprietor", in relation to any school, has the meaning given by section 114(1) of the Education Act 1944 and in Scotland has the meaning given by section 145(37) of the Education (Scotland) Act 1962;   1944 c. 31.   1962 c. 47.

"pupil" in Scotland includes a student of any age;

"retirement" includes retirement (whether voluntary or not) on grounds of age, length of service or incapacity;

"school" has the meaning given by section 114(1) of the Education Act 1944, and in Scotland has the meaning given by section 145(42) of the Education (Scotland) Act 1962;

"school education" has the meaning given by section 145(43A) of the Education (Scotland) Act 1962;

"trade" includes any business;

"training" includes any form of education or instruction;

"university" includes a university college and the college, school or hall of a university;

"upper limit of compulsory school age" means, subject to section 9 of the Education Act 1962, the age that is that limit by virtue of section 35 of the Education Act 1944 and the Order in Council made under that section;   1962 c. 12.

"woman" includes a female of any age.

(2) For the purposes of this Act two employers are to be treated as associated if one is a company of which the other (directly or indirectly) has control or if both are companies of which a third person (directly or indirectly) has control.

(3) Any power conferred by this Act to designate establishments or persons may be exercised either by naming them or by identifying them by reference to a class or other description.

(4) For the purposes of this Act a non-discrimination notice or a finding by a court or tribunal becomes final when an appeal against the notice or finding is dismissed, withdrawn or abandoned or when the time for appealing expires without an appeal having been brought; and for this purpose an appeal against a non-discrimination notice shall be taken to be dismissed if, notwithstanding that a requirement of the notice is quashed on appeal, a direction is given in respect of it under section 68(3).

PART VIII

(5) For the purposes of this Act a person is a near relative of another if that person is the wife or husband, a parent or child, a grandparent or grandchild, or a brother or sister of the other (whether of full blood or half-blood or by affinity), and " child " includes an illegitimate child and the wife or husband of an illegitimate child.

(6) Except so far as the context otherwise requires, any reference in this Act to an enactment shall be construed as a reference to that enactment as amended by or under any other enactment, including this Act.

(7) In this Act, except where otherwise indicated—
  (a) a reference to a numbered Part, section or Schedule is a reference to the Part or section of, or the Schedule to, this Act so numbered, and
  (b) a reference in a section to a numbered subsection is a reference to the subsection of that section so numbered, and
  (c) a reference in a section, subsection or Schedule to a numbered paragraph is a reference to the paragraph of that section, subsection or Schedule so numbered, and
  (d) a reference to any provision of an Act (including this Act) includes a Schedule incorporated in the Act by that provision.

Transitional and commencement provisions, amendments and repeals.

83.—(1) The provisions of Schedule 4 shall have effect for making transitional provision for the purposes of this Act.

(2) Parts II to VII shall come into operation on such day as the Secretary of State may by order appoint, and different days may be so appointed for different provisions and for different purposes.

(3) Subject to subsection (4)—
  (a) the enactments specified in Schedule 5 shall have effect subject to the amendments specified in that Schedule (being minor amendments or amendments consequential on the preceding provisions of this Act), and
  (b) the enactments specified in Schedule 6 are hereby repealed to the extent shown in column 3 of that Schedule.

(4) The Secretary of State shall by order provide for the coming into operation of the amendments contained in Schedule 5 and the repeals contained in Schedule 6, and those amendments and repeals shall have effect only as provided by an order so made.

(5) An order under this section may make such transitional provision as appears to the Secretary of State to be necessary

or expedient in connection with the provisions thereby brought into operation, including such adaptations of those provisions, or of any provisions of this Act then in operation, as appear to the Secretary of State necessary or expedient in consequence of the partial operation of this Act.

84. There shall be defrayed out of money provided by Parliament— *Financial provisions.*

    (*a*) sums required by the Secretary of State for making payments under paragraph 5 or 14 of Schedule 3, and for defraying any other expenditure falling to be made by him under or by virtue of this Act;

    (*b*) payments falling to be made under section 66(6)(*b*) or (7) in respect of the remuneration of assessors; and

    (*c*) any increase attributable to the provisions of this Act in the sums payable out of money provided by Parliament under any other Act.

85.—(1) This Act applies— *Application to Crown.*

    (*a*) to an act done by or for purposes of a Minister of the Crown or government department, or

    (*b*) to an act done on behalf of the Crown by a statutory body, or a person holding a statutory office,

as it applies to an act done by a private person.

(2) Parts II and IV apply to—

    (*a*) service for purposes of a Minister of the Crown or government department, other than service of a person holding a statutory office, or

    (*b*) service on behalf of the Crown for purposes of a person holding a statutory office or purposes of a statutory body,

as they apply to employment by a private person, and shall so apply as if references to a contract of employment included references to the terms of service.

(3) Subsections (1) and (2) have effect subject to section 17.

(4) Subsections (1) and (2) do not apply in relation to service in—

    (*a*) the naval, military or air forces of the Crown, or

    (*b*) any women's service administered by the Defence Council.

(5) Nothing in this Act shall render unlawful discrimination in admission to the Army Cadet Force, Air Training Corps,

PART VIII Sea Cadet Corps or Combined Cadet Force, or any other cadet training corps for the time being administered by the Ministry of Defence.

(6) This Act (except section 8(1) and (6)) does not apply to employment in the case of which the employee may be required to serve in support of a force or service mentioned in subsection (4)(*a*) or (*b*).

(7) Subsection (2) of section 10 shall have effect in relation to any ship, aircraft or hovercraft belonging to or possessed by Her Majesty in right of the Government of the United Kingdom as it has effect in relation to a ship, aircraft or hovercraft mentioned in paragraph (*a*) or (*b*) of that subsection, and section 10(5) shall apply accordingly.

1947 c. 44.

(8) The provisions of Parts II to IV of the Crown Proceedings Act 1947 shall apply to proceedings against the Crown under this Act as they apply to proceedings in England and Wales which by virtue of section 23 of that Act are treated for the purposes of Part II of that Act as civil proceedings by or against the Crown, except that in their application to proceedings under this Act section 20 of that Act (removal of proceedings from county court to High Court) shall not apply.

(9) The provisions of Part V of the Crown Proceedings Act 1947 shall apply to proceedings against the Crown under this Act as they apply to proceedings in Scotland which by virtue of the said Part are treated as civil proceedings by or against the Crown, except that in their application to proceedings under this Act the proviso to section 44 of that Act (removal of proceedings from the sheriff court to the Court of Session) shall not apply.

1975 c. 24.

(10) In this section " statutory body " means a body set up by or in pursuance of an enactment, and " statutory office " means an office so set up; and service " for purposes of " a Minister of the Crown or government department does not include service in any office in Schedule 2 (Ministerial offices) to the House of Commons Disqualification Act 1975 as for the time being in force.

Government appointments outside section 6.

86.—(1) This section applies to any appointment by a Minister of the Crown or government department to an office or post where section 6 does not apply in relation to the appointment.

(2) In making the appointment, and in making the arrangements for determining who should be offered the office or post,

the Minister of the Crown or government department shall not do an act which would be unlawful under section 6 if the Crown were the employer for the purposes of this Act.

PART VIII

87.—(1) This Act may be cited as the Sex Discrimination Act 1975.

Short title and extent.

(2) This Act (except paragraph 16 of Schedule 3) does not extend to Northern Ireland.

Section 8.

SCHEDULES

SCHEDULE 1

Equal Pay Act 1970

Part I

Amendments of Act

1.—(1) In section 1(6), paragraph (*b*) is repealed and the following is inserted after paragraph (*c*): "and men shall be treated as in the same employment with a woman if they are men employed by her employer or any associated employer at the same establishment or at establishments in Great Britain which include that one and at which common terms and conditions of employment are observed either generally or for employees of the relevant classes".

(2) Section 1(7) is repealed.

(3) The following is substituted for section 1(8)—

"(8) This section shall apply to—

    (*a*) service for purposes of a Minister of the Crown or government department, other than service of a person holding a statutory office, or

    (*b*) service on behalf of the Crown for purposes of a person holding a statutory office or purposes of a statutory body,

as it applies to employment by a private person, and shall so apply as if references to a contract of employment included references to the terms of service.

(9) Subsection (8) does not apply in relation to service in—

    (*a*) the naval, military or air forces of the Crown, or

    (*b*) any women's service administered by the Defence Council.

(10) In this section "statutory body" means a body set up by or in pursuance of an enactment, and "statutory office" means an office so set up; and service "for purposes of" a Minister of the Crown or government department does not include service in any office in Schedule 2 (Ministerial offices) to the House of Commons Disqualification Act 1975 as for the time being in force."

1975 c. 24.

(4) The following subsections are inserted at the end of section 1—

"(11) For the purposes of this Act it is immaterial whether the law which (apart from this subsection) is the proper law of a contract is the law of any part of the United Kingdom or not.

(12) In this Act "Great Britain" includes such of the territorial waters of the United Kingdom as are adjacent to Great Britain.

Sex Discrimination Act 1975 c. 65

Sch. 1

(13) Provisions of this section and section 2 below framed with reference to women and their treatment relative to men are to be read as applying equally in a converse case to men and their treatment relative to women ".

2.—(1) The following is substituted for section 2(1)—

" (1) Any claim in respect of the contravention of a term modified or included by virtue of an equality clause, including a claim for arrears of remuneration or damages in respect of the contravention, may be presented by way of a complaint to an industrial tribunal."

(2) After section 2(1) there is inserted—

" (1A) Where a dispute arises in relation to the effect of an equality clause the employer may apply to an industrial tribunal for an order declaring the rights of the employer and the employee in relation to the matter in question."

(3) In section 2(2)—

(*a*) for " failing to comply with their equal pay clauses " there is substituted " contravening a term modified or included by virtue of their equality clauses ", and

(*b*) after " the question may be referred by him " there is inserted " as respects all or any of them ", and

(*c*) after " claim by the women " there is inserted " or woman ".

(4) Section 2(6) is repealed.

(5) In section 2(7), the words " and there shall be paid " onwards are repealed.

3. In section 6 the following is substituted for subsection (1)—

" (1) Neither an equality clause nor the provisions of section 3(4) above shall operate in relation to terms—

(*a*) affected by compliance with the laws regulating the employment of women, or

(*b*) affording special treatment to women in connection with pregnancy or childbirth.

(1A) An equality clause and those provisions—

(*a*) shall operate in relation to terms relating to membership of an occupational pension scheme (within the meaning of the Social Security Pensions Act 1975) so far as those terms relate to any matter in respect of which the scheme has to conform with the equal access requirements of Part IV of that Act ; but

(*b*) subject to this, shall not operate in relation to terms related to death or retirement, or to any provision made in connection with death or retirement."

4. Section 8 is repealed.

5. In section 9(1), the words " Except as provided by subsection (2) below ", and sections 9(2) to (5) and 10(4) are repealed.

SCH. 1

6.—(1) For references to an equal pay clause in each place where they occur there are substituted references to an equality clause.

(2) For the words "the Industrial Court", in each place where they occur, there are substituted the words "the Industrial Arbitration Board"; in sections 4 and 10 for the words "Court" and "Court's" in each place where they occur there are substituted respectively "Board" and "Board's", and in section 5 for the word "Board" in each place where it occurs there is substituted "Agricultural Wages Board" and for the word "Court" in each place where it occurs there is substituted "Industrial Arbitration Board".

PART II

ACT AS AMENDED

1970 CHAPTER 41

An Act to prevent discrimination, as regards terms and conditions of employment, between men and women. [29th May 1970]

BE IT ENACTED by the Queen's Most Excellent Majesty, by and with the advice and consent of the Lords Spiritual and Temporal, and Commons, in this present Parliament assembled, and by the authority of the same, as follows:—

1.—(1) If the terms of a contract under which a woman is employed at an establishment in Great Britain do not include (directly or by reference to a collective agreement or otherwise) an equality clause they shall be deemed to include one.

(2) An equality clause is a provision which relates to terms (whether concerned with pay or not) of a contract under which a woman is employed (the "woman's contract"), and has the effect that—

(a) where the woman is employed on like work with a man in the same employment—

(i) if (apart from the equality clause) any term of the woman's contract is or becomes less favourable to the woman than a term of a similar kind in the contract under which that man is employed, that term of the woman's contract shall be treated as so modified as not to be less favourable, and

(ii) if (apart from the equality clause) at any time the woman's contract does not include a term corresponding to a term benefiting that man included in the contract under which he is employed, the woman's contract shall be treated as including such a term;

(b) where the woman is employed on work rated as equivalent with that of a man in the same employment—

(i) if (apart from the equality clause) any term of the

woman's contract determined by the rating of the work is or becomes less favourable to the woman than a term of a similar kind in the contract under which that man is employed, that term of the woman's contract shall be treated as so modified as not to be less favourable, and

(ii) if (apart from the equality clause) at any time the woman's contract does not include a term corresponding to a term benefiting that man included in the contract under which he is employed and determined by the rating of the work, the woman's contract shall be treated as including such a term.

(3) An equality clause shall not operate in relation to a variation between the woman's contract and the man's contract if the employer proves that the variation is genuinely due to a material difference (other than the difference of sex) between her case and his.

(4) A woman is to be regarded as employed on like work with men if, but only if, her work and theirs is of the same or a broadly similar nature, and the differences (if any) between the things she does and the things they do are not of practical importance in relation to terms and conditions of employment; and accordingly in comparing her work with theirs regard shall be had to the frequency or otherwise with which any such differences occur in practice as well as to the nature and extent of the differences.

(5) A woman is to be regarded as employed on work rated as equivalent with that of any men if, but only if, her job and their job have been given an equal value, in terms of the demand made on a worker under various headings (for instance effort, skill, decision), on a study undertaken with a view to evaluating in those terms the jobs to be done by all or any of the employees in an undertaking or group of undertakings, or would have been given an equal value but for the evaluation being made on a system setting different values for men and women on the same demand under any heading.

(6) Subject to the following subsections, for purposes of this section—

(a) " employed " means employed under a contract of service or of apprenticeship or a contract personally to execute any work or labour, and related expressions shall be construed accordingly;

. . . .

(c) two employers are to be treated as associated if one is a company of which the other (directly or indirectly) has control or if both are companies of which a third person (directly or indirectly) has control,

and men shall be treated as in the same employment with a woman if they are men employed by her employer or any associated employer at the same establishment or at establishments in Great Britain which include that one and at which common terms and conditions of employment are observed either generally or for employees of the relevant classes.

. . . .

SCH. 1

(8) This section shall apply to—
 (a) service for purposes of a Minister of the Crown or government department, other than service of a person holding a statutory office, or
 (b) service on behalf of the Crown for purposes of a person holding a statutory office or purposes of a statutory body,

as it applies to employment by a private person, and shall so apply as if references to a contract of employment included references to the terms of service.

(9) Subsection (8) does not apply in relation to service in—
 (a) the naval, military or air forces of the Crown, or
 (b) any women's service administered by the Defence Council.

1975 c. 24.

(10) In this section "statutory body" means a body set up by or in pursuance of an enactment, and "statutory office" means an office so set up; and service "for purposes of" a Minister of the Crown or government department does not include service in any office in Schedule 2 (Ministerial offices) to the House of Commons Disqualification Act 1975 as for the time being in force.

(11) For the purposes of this Act it is immaterial whether the law which (apart from this subsection) is the proper law of a contract is the law of any part of the United Kingdom or not.

(12) In this Act "Great Britain" includes such of the territorial waters of the United Kingdom as are adjacent to Great Britain.

(13) Provisions of this section and section 2 below framed with reference to women and their treatment relative to men are to be read as applying equally in a converse case to men and their treatment relative to women.

Disputes as to, and enforcement of, requirement of equal treatment.

2.—(1) Any claim in respect of the contravention of a term modified or included by virtue of an equality clause, including a claim for arrears of remuneration or damages in respect of the contravention, may be presented by way of a complaint to an industrial tribunal.

(1A) Where a dispute arises in relation to the effect of an equality clause the employer may apply to an industrial tribunal for an order declaring the rights of the employer and the employee in relation to the matter in question.

(2) Where it appears to the Secretary of State that there may be a question whether the employer of any women is or has been contravening a term modified or included by virtue of their equality clauses, but that it is not reasonable to expect them to take steps to have the question determined, the question may be referred by him as respects all or any of them to an industrial tribunal and shall be dealt with as if the reference were of a claim by the women or woman against the employer.

(3) Where it appears to the court in which any proceedings are pending that a claim or counterclaim in respect of the operation of an equality clause could more conveniently be disposed of separately by an industrial tribunal, the court may direct that the

claim or counterclaim shall be struck out; and (without prejudice to the foregoing) where in proceedings before any court a question arises as to the operation of an equality clause, the court may on the application of any party to the proceedings or otherwise refer that question, or direct it to be referred by a party to the proceedings, to an industrial tribunal for determination by the tribunal, and may stay or sist the proceedings in the meantime.

Sch. 1

(4) No claim in respect of the operation of an equality clause relating to a woman's employment shall be referred to an industrial tribunal otherwise than by virtue of subsection (3) above, if she has not been employed in the employment within the six months preceding the date of the reference.

(5) A woman shall not be entitled, in proceedings brought in respect of a failure to comply with an equality clause (including proceedings before an industrial tribunal), to be awarded any payment by way of arrears of remuneration or damages in respect of a time earlier than two years before the date on which the proceedings were instituted.

. . . .

(7) In this section "industrial tribunal" means a tribunal established under section 12 of the Industrial Training Act 1964 . . .

1964 c. 16.

3.—(1) Where a collective agreement made before or after the commencement of this Act contains any provision applying specifically to men only or to women only, the agreement may be referred, by any party to it or by the Secretary of State, to the Industrial Arbitration Board constituted under Part I of the Industrial Courts Act 1919 to declare what amendments need to be made in the agreement, in accordance with subsection (4) below, so as to remove that discrimination between men and women.

Collective agreements and pay structures.

1919 c. 69.

(2) Where on a reference under subsection (1) above the Industrial Arbitration Board have declared the amendments needing to be made in a collective agreement in accordance with that subsection, then—

(a) in so far as the terms and conditions of a person's employment are dependent on that agreement, they shall be ascertained by reference to the agreement as so amended, and any contract regulating those terms and conditions shall have effect accordingly; and

(b) if the Industrial Arbitration Board make or have made, under section 8 of the Terms and Conditions of Employment Act 1959 or any other enactment, an award or determination requiring an employer to observe the collective agreement, the award or determination shall have effect by reference to the agreement as so amended.

1959 c. 26.

(3) On a reference under subsection (1) above the Industrial Arbitration Board may direct that all or any of the amendments needing to be made in the collective agreement shall be treated as not becoming effective until a date after their decision, or as having been effective from a date before their decision but not before the reference

SCH. 1

to them, and may specify different dates for different purposes; and subsection (2) above and any such contract, award or determination as is there mentioned shall have or be deemed to have had effect accordingly.

(4) Subject to section 6 below, the amendments to be made in a collective agreement under this section shall be such as are needed—

(a) to extend to both men and women any provision applying specifically to men only or to women only; and

(b) to eliminate any resulting duplication in the provisions of the agreement in such a way as not to make the terms and conditions agreed for men, or those agreed for women, less favourable in any respect than they would have been without the amendments;

but the amendments shall not extend the operation of the collective agreement to men or to women not previously falling within it, and where accordingly a provision applying specifically to men only or to women only continues to be required for a category of men or of women (there being no provision in the agreement for women or, as the case may be, for men of that category), then the provision shall be limited to men or women of that category but there shall be made to it such amendments, if any, as are needed to secure that the terms and conditions of the men or women of that category are not in any respect less favourable than those of all persons of the other sex to whom the agreement applies.

(5) For purposes of this section " collective agreement " means any agreement as to terms and conditions of employment, being an agreement between—

(a) parties who are or represent employers or organisations of employers or associations of such organisations; and

(b) parties who are or represent organisations of employees or associations of such organisations;

but includes also any award modifying or supplementing such an agreement.

(6) Subsections (1) to (4) above (except subsection (2)(b) and subsection (3) in so far as it relates to subsection (2)(b)) shall have effect in relation to an employer's pay structure as they have effect in relation to a collective agreement, with the adaptation that a reference to the Industrial Arbitration Board may be made by the employer or by the Secretary of State; and for this purpose " pay structure " means any arrangements adopted by an employer (with or without any associated employer) which fix common terms and conditions of employment for his employees or any class of his employees, and of which the provisions are generally known or open to be known by the employees concerned.

(7) In this section the expression " employment " and related expressions, and the reference to an associated employer, shall be construed in the same way as in section 1 above, and section 1(8) shall have effect in relation to this section as well as in relation to that section.

Wages regulation orders.

4.—(1) Where a wages regulation order made before or after the commencement of this Act contains any provision applying speci-

fically to men only or to women only, the order may be referred Sch. 1
by the Secretary of State to the Industrial Arbitration Board to
declare what amendments need to be made in the order, in
accordance with the like rules as apply under section 3(4) above to
the amendment under that section of a collective agreement, so as
to remove that discrimination between men and women; and when
the Board have declared the amendments needing to be so made,
the Secretary of State may by order made by statutory instrument
coming into operation not later than five months after the date of
the Board's decision direct that (subject to any further wages regulation order) the order referred to the Board shall have effect subject
to those amendments.

(2) A wages regulation order shall be referred to the Industrial
Arbitration Board under this section if the Secretary of State is
requested so to refer it either—

(a) by a member or members of the wages council concerned
with the order who was or who were appointed as
representing employers; or

(b) by a member or members of that wages council who was
or who were appointed as representing workers;

or if in any case it appears to the Secretary of State that the order
may be amendable under this section.

(3) Where by virtue of section 12(1) of the Wages Councils Act 1959 c. 69.
1959 a contract between a worker and an employer is to have effect
with modifications specified in section 12(1), then (without prejudice
to the general saving in section 11(7) of that Act for rights conferred by or under other Acts) the contract as so modified shall
have effect subject to any further term implied by virtue of section 1
above.

(4) In this section " wages regulation order " means an order
made or having effect as if made under section 11 of the Wages
Councils Act 1959.

5.—(1) Where an agricultural wages order made before or after Agricultural
the commencement of this Act contains any provision applying wages orders.
specifically to men only or to women only, the order may be
referred by the Secretary of State to the Industrial Arbitration Board
to declare what amendments need to be made in the order, in
accordance with the like rules as apply under section 3(4) above to
the amendment under that section of a collective agreement, so as
to remove that discrimination between men and women; and when
the Industrial Arbitration Board have declared the amendments
needing to be so made, it shall be the duty of the Agricultural Wages
Board, by a further agricultural wages order coming into operation
not later than five months after the date of the Industrial Arbitration
Board's decision, either to make those amendments in the order
referred to the Industrial Arbitration Board or otherwise to replace
or amend that order so as to remove the discrimination.

(2) Where the Agricultural Wages Board certify that the effect
of an agricultural wages order is only to make such amendments
of a previous order as have under this section been declared by

SCH. 1

the Industrial Arbitration Board to be needed, or to make such amendments as aforesaid with minor modifications or modifications of limited application, or is only to revoke and reproduce with such amendments a previous order, then the Agricultural Wages Board may instead of complying with paragraphs 1 and 2 of Schedule 4, or in the case of Scotland paragraphs 1 and 2 of Schedule 3, to the Agricultural Wages Act give notice of the proposed order in such manner as appears to the Agricultural Wages Board expedient in the circumstances, and may make the order at any time after the expiration of seven days from the giving of the notice.

(3) An agricultural wages order shall be referred to the Industrial Arbitration Board under this section if the Secretary of State is requested so to refer it either—

(a) by a body for the time being entitled to nominate for membership of the Agricultural Wages Board persons representing employers (or, if provision is made for any of the persons representing employers to be elected instead of nominated, then by a member or members representing employers) ; or

(b) by a body for the time being entitled to nominate for membership of the Agricultural Wages Board persons representing workers (or, if provision is made for any of the persons representing workers to be elected instead of nominated, then by a member or members representing workers) ;

or if in any case it appears to the Secretary of State that the order may be amendable under this section.

1948 c. 47.
1949 c. 30.

(4) In this section " the Agricultural Wages Board " means the Agricultural Wages Board for England and Wales or the Scottish Agricultural Wages Board, " the Agricultural Wages Act " means the Agricultural Wages Act 1948 or the Agricultural Wages (Scotland) Act 1949 and " agricultural wages order " means an order of the Agricultural Wages Board under the Agricultural Wages Act.

Exclusion from ss. 1 to 5 of pensions etc.

6.—(1) Neither an equality clause nor the provisions of section 3(4) above shall operate in relation to terms—

(a) affected by compliance with the laws regulating the employment of women, or

(b) affording special treatment to women in connection with pregnancy or childbirth.

(1A) An equality clause and those provisions—

(a) shall operate in relation to terms relating to membership of an occupational pension scheme (within the meaning of the Social Security Pensions Act 1975) so far as those terms relate to any matter in respect of which the scheme has to conform with the equal access requirements of Part IV of that Act; but

(b) subject to this, shall not operate in relation to terms related to death or retirement, or to any provision made in connection with death or retirement.

(2) Any reference in this section to retirement includes retirement, whether voluntary or not, on grounds of age, length of service or incapacity.

SCH. 1

7.—(1) The Secretary of State or Defence Council shall not make, or recommend to Her Majesty the making of, any instrument relating to the terms and conditions of service of members of the naval, military or air forces of the Crown or of any women's service administered by the Defence Council, if the instrument has the effect of making a distinction, as regards pay, allowances or leave, between men and women who are members of those forces or of any such service, not being a distinction fairly attributable to differences between the obligations undertaken by men and those undertaken by women as such members as aforesaid.

Service pay.

(2) The Secretary of State or Defence Council may refer to the Industrial Arbitration Board for their advice any question whether a provision made or proposed to be made by any such instrument as is referred to in subsection (1) above ought to be regarded for purposes of this section as making a distinction not permitted by that subsection.

. . . .

9.—(1) . . . the foregoing provisions of this Act shall come into force on the 29th December 1975 and references in this Act to its commencement shall be construed as referring to the coming into force of those provisions on that date.

Commencemen

. . . .

10.—(1) A collective agreement, pay structure or order which after the commencement of this Act could under section 3, 4 or 5 of this Act be referred to the Industrial Arbitration Board to declare what amendments need to be made as mentioned in that section may at any time not earlier than one year before that commencement be referred to the Board under this section for their advice as to the amendments needing to be so made.

Preliminary references to Industrial Arbitration Board.

(2) A reference under this section may be made by any person authorised by section 3, 4 or 5, as the case may be, to make a corresponding reference under that section, but the Secretary of State shall not under this section refer an order to the Industrial Arbitration Board unless requested so to do as mentioned in section 4(2) or 5(3), as the case may be, nor be required to refer an order if so requested.

(3) A collective agreement, pay structure or order referred to the Industrial Arbitration Board under this section may after the commencement of this Act be again referred to the Board under section 3, 4 or 5 ; but at that commencement any reference under this section (if still pending) shall lapse.

. . . .

SCH. 1
Short title, interpretation and extent.

11.—(1) This Act may be cited as the Equal Pay Act 1970.

(2) In this Act the expressions "man" and "woman" shall be read as applying to persons of whatever age.

(3) This Act shall not extend to Northern Ireland.

Section 27.

SCHEDULE 2

TRANSITIONAL EXEMPTION ORDERS FOR EDUCATIONAL ADMISSIONS

Public sector (England and Wales)

1944 c. 31.
1968 c. 17.

1. Where under section 13 of the Education Act 1944 (as set out in Schedule 3 to the Education Act 1968) a responsible body submits to the Secretary of State, in accordance with subsection (1) or (2) of that section, proposals for an alteration in its admissions arrangements such as is mentioned in section 27(1) of this Act the submission of those proposals shall be treated as an application for the making by the Secretary of State of a transitional exemption order, and if he thinks fit the Secretary of State may make the order accordingly.

2. Regulations under section 33 of the Education Act 1944 may provide for the submission to the Secretary of State of an application for the making by him of a transitional exemption order in relation to a special school, and for the making by him of the order.

3. Regulations under section 100 of the Education Act 1944 may provide for the submission to the Secretary of State of an application for the making by him of a transitional exemption order in relation to an establishment—

   (a) which is designated under section 24(1), and

   (b) in respect of which grants are payable under subsection (1)(b) of the said section 100,

and for the making by him of the order.

1974 c. 7.

4. Regulations under section 5(2) of the Local Government Act 1974 may provide for the submission to the Secretary of State of an application for the making by him of a transitional exemption order in relation to any educational establishment maintained by a local education authority and not falling within paragraphs 1 to 3, and for the making by him of the order.

Private sector (England and Wales)

5.—(1) In the case of an establishment in England or Wales not falling within paragraphs 1 to 4 the responsible body may submit to the Equal Opportunities Commission set up under Part VI an application for the making by the Commission of a transitional exemption order in relation to the establishment, and if they think fit the Commission may make the order accordingly.

(2) An application under this paragraph shall specify the transitional period proposed by the responsible body to be provided for in the order, the stages by which within that period the body proposes to move to the position where section 22(b) is complied with, and any other matters relevant to the terms and operation of the order applied for.

(3) The Commission shall not make an order on an application under this paragraph unless they are satisfied that the terms of the application are reasonable having regard to the nature of the premises at which the establishment is carried on, the accommodation, equipment and facilities available, and the financial resources of the responsible body.

Public and private sectors (Scotland)

6. Any application for a transitional exemption order made by the responsible body in relation to an establishment falling within paragraph 6 or 7 of the Table in section 22 shall be made to the Secretary of State, and in relation to an establishment falling within paragraphs 8, 9 and 10 of that Table shall be made to the Equal Opportunities Commission.

7. An application under paragraph 6 shall specify the transitional period proposed by the responsible body to be provided for in the order, the stages by which within that period the body proposes to move to the position where section 22(*b*) is complied with, and any other matters relevant to the terms and operation of the order applied for.

8. The Secretary of State on any application under paragraph 6 may make a transitional exemption order on such terms and conditions as he may think fit.

9. The Commission on any application under paragraph 6 may if they think fit make a transitional exemption order, but shall not make such an order unless they are satisfied that the terms of the application are reasonable having regard to the nature of the premises at which the establishment is carried on, the accommodation, equipment and facilities available, and the financial resources of the responsible body.

SCHEDULE 3

EQUAL OPPORTUNITIES COMMISSION

Incorporation and status

1. On the appointment by the Secretary of State of the first Commissioners, the Commission shall come into existence as a body corporate with perpetual succession and a common seal.

2.—(1) The Commission is not an emanation of the Crown, and shall not act or be treated as the servant or agent of the Crown.

(2) Accordingly—
  (*a*) neither the Commission nor a Commissioner or member of its staff as such is entitled to any status, immunity, privilege or exemption enjoyed by the Crown;
  (*b*) the Commissioners and members of the staff of the Commission as such are not civil servants; and
  (*c*) the Commission's property is not property of, or held on behalf of, the Crown.

Tenure of office of Commissioners

3.—(1) A Commissioner shall hold and vacate his office in accordance with the terms of his appointment.

(2) A person shall not be appointed a Commissioner for more than five years.

(3) With the consent of the Commissioner concerned, the Secretary of State may alter the terms of an appointment so as to make a full-time Commissioner into a part-time Commissioner or vice versa, or for any other purpose.

(4) A Commissioner may resign by notice to the Secretary of State.

(5) The Secretary of State may terminate the appointment of a Commissioner if satisfied that—

(a) without the consent of the Commission, he failed to attend the meetings of the Commission during a continuous period of six months beginning not earlier than nine months before the termination; or

(b) he is an undischarged bankrupt, or has made an arrangement with his creditors, or is insolvent within the meaning of paragraph 9(2) of Schedule 3 to the Conveyancing and Feudal Reform (Scotland) Act 1970; or

(c) he is by reason of physical or mental illness, or for any other reason, incapable of carrying out his duties.

(6) Past service as a Commissioner is no bar to re-appointment.

Tenure of office of chairman and deputy chairmen

4.—(1) The chairman and each deputy chairman shall hold and vacate his office in accordance with the terms of his appointment, and may resign by notice to the Secretary of State.

(2) The office of the chairman or a deputy chairman is vacated if he ceases to be a Commissioner.

(3) Past service as chairman or a deputy chairman is no bar to re-appointment.

Remuneration of Commissioners

5. The Secretary of State may pay, or make such payments towards the provision of, such remuneration, pensions, allowances or gratuities to or in respect of the Commissioners or any of them as, with the consent of the Minister for the Civil Service, he may determine.

6. Where a person ceases to be a Commissioner otherwise than on the expiry of his term of office, and it appears to the Secretary of State that there are special circumstances which make it right for that person to receive compensation, the Secretary of State may with the consent of the Minister for the Civil Service direct the Commission to make to that person a payment of such amount as, with the consent of that Minister, the Secretary of State may determine.

Additional Commissioners

7.—(1) Paragraphs 2(2), 3(1) and (6), and 6 shall apply to additional Commissioners appointed under section 57(2) as they apply to Commissioners.

(2) The Commission may pay, or make such payments towards the provision of, such remuneration, pensions, allowances or gratuities to or in respect of an additional Commissioner as the Secretary of State, with the consent of the Minister for the Civil Service, may determine.

SCH. 3

(3) With the approval of the Secretary of State and the consent of the additional Commissioner concerned, the Commission may alter the terms of an appointment of an additional Commissioner so as to make a full-time additional Commissioner into a part-time additional Commissioner or vice versa, or for any other purpose.

(4) An additional Commissioner may resign by notice to the Commission.

(5) The Secretary of State, or the Commission acting with the approval of the Secretary of State, may terminate the appointment of an additional Commissioner if satisfied that—

(a) without reasonable excuse he failed to carry out the duties for which he was appointed during a continuous period of three months beginning not earlier than six months before the termination ; or

(b) he is a person such as is mentioned in paragraph 3(5)(b); or

(c) he is by reason of physical or mental illness, or for any other reason, incapable of carrying out his duties.

(6) The appointment of an additional Commissioner shall terminate at the conclusion of the investigation for which he was appointed, if not sooner.

Staff

8. The Commission may, after consultation with the Secretary of State, appoint such officers and servants as they think fit, subject to the approval of the Minister for the Civil Service as to numbers and as to remuneration and other terms and conditions of service.

9.—(1) Employment with the Commission shall be included among the kinds of employment to which a superannuation scheme under section 1 of the Superannuation Act 1972 can apply, and accordingly in Schedule 1 to that Act (in which those kinds of employment are listed) the words " Equal Opportunities Commission " shall be inserted at the appropriate place in alphabetical order.

1972 c. 11.

(2) Where a person who is employed by the Commission and is by reference to that employment a participant in a scheme under section 1 of the Superannuation Act 1972 becomes a Commissioner or an additional Commissioner, the Minister for the Civil Service may determine that his service as a Commissioner or additional Commissioner shall be treated for the purposes of the scheme as service as an employee of the Commission ; and his rights under the scheme shall not be affected by paragraph 5 or 7(2).

10. The Employers' Liability (Compulsory Insurance) Act 1969 shall not require insurance to be effected by the Commission.

1969 c. 57.

SCH. 3

Proceedings and business

11.—(1) Subject to the provisions of this Act, the Commission may make arrangements for the regulation of their proceedings and business, and may vary or revoke those arrangements.

(2) The arrangements may, with the approval of the Secretary of State, provide for the discharge under the general direction of the Commission of any of the Commission's functions by a committee of the Commission, or by two or more Commissioners.

(3) Anything done by or in relation to a committee, or Commissioners, in the discharge of the Commission's functions shall have the same effect as if done by or in relation to the Commission.

12. The validity of any proceedings of the Commission shall not be affected by any vacancy among the members of the Commission or by any defect in the appointment of any Commissioner or additional Commissioner.

13. The quorum for meetings of the Commission shall in the first instance be determined by a meeting of the Commission attended by not less than five Commissioners.

Finance

14. The Secretary of State shall pay to the Commission expenses incurred or to be incurred by it under paragraphs 6, 7 and 8, and, with the consent of the Minister for the Civil Service and the Treasury, shall pay to the Commission such sums as the Secretary of State thinks fit for enabling the Commission to meet other expenses.

15.—(1) The Commission shall keep proper accounts of their income and expenditure, and shall prepare and send to the Secretary of State statements of account in relation to each financial year of the Commission.

(2) The financial year of the Commission shall be the twelve months ending on 31st March.

Disqualification Acts

1975 c. 24.
1975 c. 25.

16.—(1) In Part II of Schedule 1 to the House of Commons Disqualification Act 1975 and Part II of Schedule 1 to the Northern Ireland Assembly Disqualification Act 1975 (bodies of which all members are disqualified under those Acts) there shall (at the appropriate place in alphabetical order) be inserted the following entry:—

" The Equal Opportunities Commission ".

(2) In Part III of Schedule 1 to each of those Acts of 1975 (other disqualifying offices) there shall (at the appropriate place in alphabetical order) be inserted the following entry:—

" Additional Commissioner of the Equal Opportunities Commission ".

SCHEDULE 4

Section 83.

TRANSITIONAL PROVISIONS

1. Section 12 does not apply, as respects any organisation,—

   (a) to contributions or other payments falling to be made to the organisation by its members or by persons seeking membership, or

   (b) to financial benefits accruing to members of the organisation by reason of their membership,

where the payment falls to be made, or the benefit accrues, before 1st January 1978 under rules of the organisation made before the passing of this Act.

2. Until 1st January 1978, section 12(2) does not apply to any organisation of members of the teaching profession where at the passing of this Act—

   (a) the organisation is an incorporated company with articles of association, and

   (b) the articles of association restrict membership to persons of one sex (disregarding any minor exceptions), and

   (c) there exists another organisation within paragraphs (a) and (b) which is for persons of the opposite sex and has objects, as set out in the memorandum of association, which are substantially the same as those of the first mentioned organisation, subject only to differences consequential on the difference of sex.

3.—(1) Until a date specified by order made by the Secretary of State the courses of training to be undergone by men as a condition of the issue of certificates to them under the Midwives Act 1951 or the Midwives (Scotland) Act 1951 (as amended by section 20) must be courses approved in writing by or on behalf of the Secretary of State for the purposes of this paragraph. 1951 c. 53. 1951 c. 54.

(2) Until the date specified under sub-paragraph (1), section 9 of the Midwives Act 1951 and section 10 of the Midwives (Scotland) Act 1951 (regulation of persons other than certified midwives attending women in childbirth) shall have effect as if for the words from the beginning to (but not including) " attends a woman in childbirth " where they first occur there were substituted the words—

   " If a person other than—

   (a) a woman who is a certified midwife, or

   (b) in a place approved in writing by or on behalf of the Secretary of State a man who is a certified midwife ".

The amendment made by this sub-paragraph shall be read without regard to the sections 35A and 37A inserted in the said Acts of 1951 by section 20(4) and (5).

(3) On and after the said date the words to be substituted for those, in the said sections 9 and 10, mentioned in sub-paragraph (2) are—

SCH. 4

1946 c. 36.

"If a person who is not a certified midwife".

(4) An order under this paragraph shall be laid in draft before each House of Parliament, and section 6(1) of the Statutory Instruments Act 1946 (Parliamentary control by negative resolution of draft instruments) shall apply accordingly.

4.—(1) If the responsible body for any educational establishment which (apart from this sub-paragraph) would be required to comply with the provisions of section 22(b), and of section 25 so far as they apply to acts to which section 22(b) relates, from the commencement of those provisions, is of the opinion that it would be impracticable for it to do so, it may before that commencement apply for an order authorising discriminatory admissions during the transitional period specified in the order.

(2) Section 27(2) to (5) and Schedule 2 shall apply for the purposes of sub-paragraph (1) as they apply in relation to transitional exemption orders.

1970 c. 41.

5.—(1) Section 6 of the Equal Pay Act 1970 (as amended by paragraph 3 of Schedule 1 to this Act) shall apply as if the references to death or retirement in subsection (1A)(b) of the said section 6 included references to sums payable on marriage in pursuance of a contract of employment made before the passing of this Act, or the commutation, at any time, of the right to such sums.

(2) In relation to service within section 1(8) of the said Act of 1970 (service of the Crown) for the reference in this paragraph to a contract of employment made before the passing of this Act there shall be substituted a reference to terms of service entered into before the passing of this Act.

Section 83.

SCHEDULE 5

MINOR AND CONSEQUENTIAL AMENDMENTS

Factories Act 1961 (c. 34)

1. In section 15(2) (unfenced machinery: operations carried out by specified male persons) the word "male" shall be omitted.

The Registration of Births, Deaths and Marriages (Scotland) Act 1965 (c. 49)

2. In section 21(6) for the word "woman" there shall be substituted the word "person".

Health and Safety at Work etc. Act 1974 (c. 37)

3. In Schedule 1, after the entry relating to the Emergency Laws (Miscellaneous Provisions) Act 1953, there is inserted the following—

| 1954 c. 57. | The Baking Industry (Hours of Work) Act 1954. | The whole Act. |

Trade Union and Labour Relations Act 1974 (*c.* 52)   Sch. 5

4. In Schedule 1, in paragraph 26(1), after " paragraph " there is inserted " and in section 64 of the Sex Discrimination Act 1975 ".

SCHEDULE 6
Section 83.
Further Repeals

Session and Chapter	Short Title	Extent of Repeal
7 & 8 Geo. 6. c. 31.	Education Act 1944.	Section 24(3).
14 & 15 Geo. 6. c. 53.	Midwives Act 1951.	In section 11(1), the words " or a male person ".
10 & 11 Eliz. 2. c. 47.	Education (Scotland) Act 1962.	Section 82(2).

PRODUCED IN ENGLAND BY SWIFT PRINTERS LTD.
FOR HAROLD GLOVER

Controller of Her Majesty's Stationery Office and Queen's Printer of Acts of Parliament

Third impression (with corrections) March 1976

CORRECTIONS

Errors appear in the first impression (November 1975) of this Act and the following corrections have been incorporated into this reprint.

Page iv, Section 78,
    for " Charities "
    read " charities "

Page 1, Section 1(1)(*b*), line 1,
    for " on "
    read " or "

Page 27, Section 43(3), line 1,
    for " in England "
    read " to England "

Page 63, subsection (6)(*c*), line 4,
    for " control."
    read " control,"

Page 64, subsection (8)(*b*), line 2,
    delete " " "

Page 64, Section 2(3), line 2,

Page 65, Section 2(3), line 1,
    for " counter-claim "
    read " counterclaim "